Sample Pages

Illustrations of Organization and Research Techniques in Thomson Reuters

Key Number Digests
National Reporter System
U.S.C.A. and Other West Statutes
American Jurisprudence 2d
American Law Reports
Words and Phrases
Black's Law Dictionary

Designed for Classroom Use in
All Courses on Legal Research

Reprinted from Copyrighted Publications
of Thomson Reuters,
Copyright 2014

ISBN: 978-0-314-67673-3

Fifth Edition

By The Publisher's Editorial Staff

 THOMSON REUTERS™

Mat. #41705167

Outline of Legal Reference Material

Primary Sources

Statutes
    Constitutions
    Treaties ───────────────▶
    Federal Statutes

> Statutes at Large
> U.S. Code and Westlaw and WestlawNext
> U.S. Code Annotated
> U.S. Code Service

    State Statutes ───────────▶

> Session Laws, etc.
> Compiled Statutes, Revised Statutes
> Codes, etc.
> Westlaw and WestlawNext

    Municipal Ordinances
    Rules of Administrative Bodies
    Rules of Court
    Executive Orders and Promulgations

Decisions
    United States Supreme Court Reports ──▶
    Federal Cases (to 1880)
    Federal Reporter (1880 to date)
        (National Reporter System) and Westlaw
        and WestlawNext)

> Government Series
> Lawyer's Edition
> Supreme Court Reporter (National
>   Reporter System)
> Westlaw and WestlawNext

    Federal Supplement (1932 to date)
        (National Reporter System) and Westlaw
        and WestlawNext
    Federal Rules Decisions (National Reporter
        System) and Westlaw and WestlawNext
    State Reports, Westlaw and WestlawNext

    National Reporter System ───────▶

> Supreme Court Reporter
> Federal Reporter
> Federal Supplement
> Federal Rules Decisions
> Federal Appendix
> Atlantic Reporter
> North Eastern Reporter
> North Western Reporter
> Pacific Reporter
> South Eastern Reporter
> Southern Reporter
> South Western Reporter
> California Reporter
> New York Supplement
> Military Justice Reporter
> Westlaw and WestlawNext

    Selected Reports ───────────▶

> American Law Reports
> ALR Federal

    Subject or Special Reports ────────▶

> American Maritime Cases
> West's Bankruptcy Reporter
> Education Law Reporter
> Federal Rules Service
> Federal Rules of Evidence Service
> West's American Tribal Law Reporter
> Uniform Commercial Code Reporting
>   Service
> Social Security Reporter
> Military Justice Reporter
> Miller's Standard Insurance Policies
>   Annotated
> Westlaw and WestlawNext

    Decisions of Administrative Bodies ────▶

> Interstate Commerce Commission
> Federal Trade Commission
> Federal Aviation Decisions
> West's Veterans Appeals Reporter
> Westlaw and WestlawNext

Secondary Sources

Encyclopedia ─────────────────────▶ | American Jurisprudence 2d
Words and Phrases
Textbooks
Treatises
Practioner's Handbooks
Loose Leaf Services
Legal Dictionaries
Citation Books
Legal Thesauruses
Law Reviews
Westlaw and WestlawNext

Finding Tools

Digests
    American Digest System
        Century Digest   1658 to 1896
        First Decennial Digest   1897 to 1906
        Second Decennial Digest   1907 to 1916
        Third Decennial Digest   1916 to 1926
        Fourth Decennial Digest   1926 to 1936
        Fifth Decennial Digest   1936 to 1946
        Sixth Decennial Digest   1946 to 1956
        Seventh Decennial Digest   1956 to 1966
        Eighth Decennial Digest   1966 to 1976
        Ninth Decennial Digest, Part I 1976 to 1981
        Ninth Decennial Digest, Part II 1981 to 1986
        Tenth Decennial Digest, Part I 1986 to 1991
        Tenth Decennial Digest, Part II 1991 to 1996
        Eleventh Decennial Digest, Part I 1996 to 2001
        Eleventh Decennial Digest, Part II 2001 to 2004
        Eleventh Decennial Digest, Part III 2004 to 2007
        Twelfth Decennial Digest, Part I 2008 to 2010
        Twelfth Decennial Digest, Part II 2010 to 2013
        General Digest   2013 to Present
    Other Digests
        Supreme Court Digest
        Federal Practice Digest
        State and Reporter Digests
        Selected Case Series Digests
        Subject or Special Reports Digest
        Westlaw and WestlawNext
    Tables of
        Cases Reported
        Cases Digested, Plaintiff
        Cases Digested, Defendant
        Cases Affirmed, Reversed, or Modified
        Cases Cited, by Popular Name,
        Cases Cited
        Parallel Citations
        Statutes Construed
    Other
        Indexes to Legal Periodicals

Computer Assisted Legal Research
    Westlaw and WestlawNext

Contents

Introduction

This workbook provides pages from major Thomson Reuters publications, along with problems to illustrate the use of those publications.

"How to Analyze Fact Situations" is a suggested framework for you to use to analyze facts and isolate words or concepts important to your research.

The Outline of Legal Reference Material indicates the organization of reference sources into three main categories. They are:

- Primary Sources: materials containing the text of the law such as cases from federal or state courts or statutes passed by legislatures;

- Secondary Sources: books such as encyclopedias, dictionaries and treatises which explain and comment on the law; and

- Finding Tools: such as digests which help you find material pertinent to your research problem.

When you research legal issues you are often confronted with a multitude of facts but minimal direction. In order to successfully complete your research you need to sift through the facts and concepts and decide which are most important to your research. The technique suggested below is one many researchers use successfully. It can be used for the sample problems in the chapters on Digests, USCA, Am Jur 2d, and American Law Reports.

How to Analyze Facts

When analyzing your fact situation for the purpose of searching for cases or statutes on point, it is a good plan to ask yourself "What words describe the parties concerned; the places or things involved; the basis of action or issue; the possible defenses and the relief sought."

1. Parties

Parties should be understood to be persons of a particular class, occupation or relation; e.g., children, collectors, heirs, or any person who is either directly or indirectly necessary to a proper determination of the action.

2. Places and Things

Places and Things should be understood as being objects which necessarily must exist before any cause of action or dispute can arise; objects perceptible through the senses; e.g., automobiles, sidewalks, derricks or garages are words describing the places or things which must exist before a cause of action alleging negligent use or defective condition can arise regarding them.

3. Basis of Action or Issue

Basis of action or issue should be understood as being some wrong suffered by another's neglect of duty; e.g., loss (of goods); some affirmative wrong—boycott, ejection, assault; some legal obligation ignored—stop, look and listen or the infraction of some statutory or constitutional provision—eight-hour law, the Sherman Act.

4. Defense

Defense should be understood as being some reason in law or fact why plaintiff should not recover; e.g., failure of consideration, act of God, assumption of risk, infancy.

5. Relief Sought

Relief sought should be understood as being the legal remedy sought; e.g., restraining order, restoration damages, annulment.

1. West Digests

The Digest chapter illustrates the use of West's classification system to find cases dealing with your legal issue. The goal is to find Key Numbers that will link you to the correct location in case law digests.

Digest Problem:

A creditor with a security interest in an automobile would like to repossess the automobile. However, the creditor has heard that the debtor has filed for bankruptcy relief. Can the creditor still repossess the automobile?

First step:

To adequately search the digests, we will need to determine an appropriate Key Number.

First, a little background on the Key Number System (KNS). The KNS breaks the entire universe of caselaw into about 400 major topics, such as Contracts, Criminal Law, Patents, etc. Each of those topics is further subdivided in individual points of law called Key Numbers. There are over 100,000 classifiable Key Numbers.

One option for finding a relevant Key Number is to look at the Descriptive-Word Index (known as the DWI). The DWI, which is a print publication that accompanies most digest sets, contains a list of words or phrases, along with the Key Number(s) that most likely correspond to the legal issues presented by those words or phrases. Page 4 contains a page from the DWI for West's Federal Practice Digest, showing that points about repossession as violative of the automatic stay in bankruptcy classify to Bankruptcy ☞ 2400.

Another option is to peruse the Key Number outline. You can find the outline either in a one-volume book entitled West's Analysis of American Law, or in the Digests (the relevant portion of the outline precedes each Topic in the Digests). If you look at the Bankruptcy topic, you will notice that there is a section IV named Effect of Bankruptcy Relief; Injunction and Stay. Section IV has a subsection B named Automatic Stay. Within that subsection B is a Key Number called 2400—Repossession. A page from West's Analysis of American Law can be found at page 6. A page from the Bankruptcy outline in West's Federal Practice Digest can be found at page 8.

WEST'S
FEDERAL PRACTICE
DIGEST 4th

Volume 97

DESCRIPTIVE - WORD INDEX
A — CI

WEST GROUP
A THOMSON COMPANY

3

BANKRUPTCY—Cont'd

REMAND, Bankr ☞ 2090, 2091
Appeal from bankruptcy court, Bankr ☞ 3790

REMOVAL,
Trustee, Bankr ☞ 3007

REMOVAL of cases, Bankr ☞ 2086.1-2089
Remand, Bankr ☞ 2090, 2091

RENT,
Administrative claim, Bankr ☞ 2876
Payments in ordinary course of business, Bankr ☞ 2616(8)

RENT lien,
Avoidability, Bankr ☞ 2581

REOPENING case, Bankr ☞ 3444-3444.60
Generally, Bankr ☞ 3444.10
Conditions, Bankr ☞ 3444.40
Discretion, Bankr ☞ 3444.20
Effect, Bankr ☞ 3444.60
Evidence, Bankr ☞ 3444.50(4)
Grounds and objections,
Generally, Bankr ☞ 3444.30(1)
Fraud or collusion, Bankr ☞ 3444.30(7)
Lien avoidance, Bankr ☞ 3444.30(4)
No-asset cases, Bankr ☞ 3444.30(6)
Omitted creditors, Bankr ☞ 3444.30(3)
Prejudice or harm to creditors, Bankr ☞ 3444.30(5)
State court determinations, Bankr ☞ 3444.30(8)
Unadministered assets, Bankr ☞ 3444.30(2)
Laches, Bankr ☞ 3444.50(3)
Standing, Bankr ☞ 3444.50(2)
Sua sponte determination, Bankr ☞ 3444.50(2)

REORGANIZATION. See heading CHAPTER 11, generally.

REPLACEMENT lien, adequate protection, relief from stay, Bankr ☞ 2434

REPORTS, Bankr ☞ 3011

REPOSSESSION, automatic stay, Bankr ☞ 2400

RES JUDICATA,
Finality of judgment, Judgm ☞ 663

RESEARCH,
Attorneys, documentation and itemization, Bankr ☞ 3203(4)

RESIDENCE,
Exemption, Bankr ☞ 2774
Lien avoidance, Bankr ☞ 2792

BANKRUPTCY—Cont'd

RESTITUTION,
Dischargeability of liability for restitution imposed on criminal conviction, Bankr ☞ 3359

RESTRAINING orders, Bankr ☞ 2374

RETIREMENT and pensions. See subheading PENSION under this heading.

RETROACTIVITY, statutes, Bankr ☞ 2023-2025

REVERSION of surplus to debtor, Bankr ☞ 3445

REVIEW. See subheading APPEAL and error under this heading.

REVOCATION,
Abandonment of property, Bankr ☞ 3136
Discharge, Bankr ☞ 3320-3322

RIGHTS of action,
Estate property, Bankr ☞ 2552-2556

RULE of explicitness, subordination, Bankr ☞ 2970

RULES, Bankr ☞ 2129

SALE of estate property, Bankr ☞ 3067.1-3081
Generally, Bankr ☞ 3067.1
Adequate protection, sale free of liens, Bankr ☞ 3073
Application of proceeds, Bankr ☞ 3078(1-3)
Appraisal, Bankr ☞ 3072(2)
Collateral attack, Bankr ☞ 3081
Conclusiveness absent stay on appeal, Bankr ☞ 3776.5(5)
Confirmation, Bankr ☞ 3070, 3075
Conveyance and delivery, Bankr ☞ 3076
Course of business, sale outside, Bankr ☞ 3069
Emergency sale, Bankr ☞ 3069
Encumbered property, Bankr ☞ 3068
Expense, liability of security, Bankr ☞ 2854(4)
Joint interests, Bankr ☞ 3068
Liabilities of purchasers, Bankr ☞ 3079
Liens,
Application of proceeds, Bankr ☞ 3078(2)
Sale free of, Bankr ☞ 3073
Limited interests, Bankr ☞ 3068
Manner and terms, Bankr ☞ 3072(1, 2)
Mortgages, application of proceeds, Bankr ☞ 3078(3)
Nonprice factors, Bankr ☞ 3075
Notice, Bankr ☞ 3071

WEST'S

ANALYSIS OF

AMERICAN LAW

2013 Edition

WITH KEY NUMBER CLASSIFICATIONS

 THOMSON REUTERS™

51. BANKRUPTCY

WEST'S
FEDERAL PRACTICE
DIGEST 5th

Volume 38

BANKRUPTCY  **2341 to 2420**

Mat # 41271361

8

Once you determine the likely Key Number, you can go into a Digest to find headnotes assigned to that Key Number. The KNS topics are arranged alphabetically in a Digest, and the Key Numbers are in numerical order. The various Digests are listed on page iii.

A good place to look for bankruptcy materials would be West's Federal Practice Digest, since most bankruptcy-related issues arise in federal court. The Federal Practice Digest is now entering the 5th series, which encompasses cases from 2003 to present. An example from the West's Federal Practice Digest 5th containing headnotes assigned to Bankruptcy ☞ 2400 can be found at pages 11–12. If you want to see headnotes from cases preceding 2003, you can work through earlier series of the West's Federal Practice Digest. An example from the 4th series can be found at page 14.

Another good digest choice would be West's Bankruptcy Digest. An example from that Digest containing headnotes assigned to Bankruptcy ☞ 2400 can be found at page 16.

If you are interested in finding a comprehensive digest containing both federal and state cases, look at the Decennial Digest. The most recent version of the Decennial Digest is the Twelfth Decennial Digest, Part 2. An example from that Digest containing headnotes assigned to Bankruptcy ☞ 2400 can be found at page 18. Earlier cases can be found in prior versions of the Decennial Digest. A complete list of the Decennial Digest versions can be found on page iii.

If you are interested only in cases arising out of a specific state, look at the digest for that specific state. A state digest, such as West's California Digest 2d, will cover cases from that state's courts, as well as federal cases that originated in federal courts for that state. An example from West's California Digest 2d containing headnotes assigned to Bankruptcy ☞ 2400 can be found at page 20.

Digests will include "pocket parts" for recent material added since the time that the bound volume was last recompiled. A "pocket part" is a pamphlet tucked into the inside back cover of a bound volume. Sometimes, if a "pocket part" becomes too large, a stand-alone supplementary pamphlet will be issued in lieu of a pocket part. Always check the "pocket part" (or supplementary pamphlet) for the most recent cases. An example of a "pocket part" from West's Federal Practice Digest 5th containing a headnote from Bankruptcy ☞ 2400 can be found at page 22.

WEST'S
FEDERAL PRACTICE
DIGEST 5th

Volume 38

BANKRUPTCY ⟜ 2341 to 2420

Mat # 41271361

prepetition obligations. Bankr.Code, 11 U.S.C.A. § 362(a)(3–7).

    In re All Trac Transp., Inc., 306 B.R. 859, subsequent determination 310 B.R. 570, affirmed 2005 WL 5012640, affirmed 223 Fed.Appx. 299, affirmed 2005 WL 5012640, affirmed 223 Fed.Appx. 299.

Recoupment by a creditor does not violate the automatic stay. Bankr.Code, 11 U.S.C.A. § 362(a).

    In re All Trac Transp., Inc., 306 B.R. 859, subsequent determination 310 B.R. 570, affirmed 2005 WL 5012640, affirmed 223 Fed.Appx. 299, affirmed 2005 WL 5012640, affirmed 223 Fed.Appx. 299.

Automatic stay applies to setoff by a creditor. Bankr.Code, 11 U.S.C.A. § 362(a).

    In re All Trac Transp., Inc., 306 B.R. 859, subsequent determination 310 B.R. 570, affirmed 2005 WL 5012640, affirmed 223 Fed.Appx. 299, affirmed 2005 WL 5012640, affirmed 223 Fed.Appx. 299.

Recoupment did not apply to shield, from the automatic stay, bank's application of postpetition funds to Chapter 11 debtor-trucking company's prepetition debts; funds collected by bank on purchased accounts receivable under parties' factoring agreement derived from a transaction separate from debtor's obligations for purchase of fuel under parties' fuel agreement, and, similarly, funds collected by bank pursuant to factoring agreement derived from a transaction separate from debtor's obligations for bank's license fee advance negotiated by a separate agreement outside the ordinary course of the factoring agreement. Bankr.Code, 11 U.S.C.A. § 362(a).

    In re All Trac Transp., Inc., 306 B.R. 859, subsequent determination 310 B.R. 570, affirmed 2005 WL 5012640, affirmed 223 Fed.Appx. 299, affirmed 2005 WL 5012640, affirmed 223 Fed.Appx. 299.

Bank's application of balance of Chapter 11 debtor's demand account to debtor's prepetition line of credit with bank violated the automatic stay. Bankr.Code, 11 U.S.C.A. § 362(a).

    In re All Trac Transp., Inc., 306 B.R. 859, subsequent determination 310 B.R. 570, affirmed 2005 WL 5012640, affirmed 223 Fed.Appx. 299, affirmed 2005 WL 5012640, affirmed 223 Fed.Appx. 299.

Bkrtcy.N.D.Tex. 2003. Governmental entity was not a "person," and thus could not qualify as "forward contract merchant," of kind entitled to exercise right of setoff postpetition under statutory exception to automatic stay. Bankr.Code, 11 U.S.C.A. §§ 101(26), 41), 362(b)(6), 556.

    In re Mirant Corp., 303 B.R. 319.

Bkrtcy.S.D.Tex. 2005. Administrative freeze, placed on debtors' bank account by financial institution upon learning of Chapter 7 petition while awaiting decision from trustee as to disposition of funds, did not violate automatic stay provision that prohibited setoff of any debt owing to debtor that arose before commencement of case against any claim against debtor, since institution was not creditor and therefore had no set off rights; institution could not violate statute when very circumstances proscribed by statute were not present. 11 U.S.C.A. § 362(a)(7).

    In re Calvin, 329 B.R. 589.

Bkrtcy.W.D.Va. 2006. Regardless of any established right to conduct setoff that creditor may have under nonbankruptcy law, postpetition acts to conduct setoff are prohibited by automatic stay. 11 U.S.C.A. § 362(a)(7).

    In re Moore, 350 B.R. 650.

⌖2400. —— Repossession.

C.A.11 (Ga.) 2004. Where, under Georgia law, legal title and right of redemption remained with Chapter 13 debtor even after secured creditor had lawfully repossessed motor vehicle securing its claim prepetition, motor vehicle was included in "property of the estate" and was protected by automatic stay; on petition date, creditor had not yet complied with disposition or retention procedures of the Georgia Uniform Commercial Code (U.C.C.). Bankr.Code, 11 U.S.C.A. §§ 362(a), 541(a); West's Ga.Code Ann. § 11-9-101 et seq.

    In re Rozier, 376 F.3d 1323.

C.A.11 (Ga.) 2003. To extent that, following creditor's repossession of motor vehicle securing its claim, both legal title to vehicle and right of redemption remained with debtor under governing Georgia law, vehicle was included in "property of the estate" when debtor later filed for Chapter 13 relief, and was protected by automatic stay. Bankr.Code, 11 U.S.C.A. §§ 362, 541(a)(1).

    In re Rozier, 348 F.3d 1305, certified question answered Motors Acceptance Corp. v. Rozier, 597 S.E.2d 367, 278 Ga. 52, answer to certified question conformed to 376 F.3d 1323.

To extent that, following creditor's repossession of motor vehicle securing its claim, legal title passed to creditor under governing Georgia law and debtor retained only a right of redemption, vehicle was not included in "property of the estate" when debtor later filed for Chapter 13 relief, and was not protected by automatic

† **This Case was not selected for publication in the National Reporter System**
For cited U.S.C.A. sections and legislative history, see United States Code Annotated

stay. Bankr.Code, 11 U.S.C.A. §§ 362, 541(a)(1).

In re Rozier, 348 F.3d 1305, certified question answered Motors Acceptance Corp. v. Rozier, 597 S.E.2d 367, 278 Ga. 52, answer to certified question conformed to 376 F.3d 1323.

C.A.7 (Ill.) 2009. Secured creditor that had repossessed Chapter 13 debtor's vehicle prepetition "exercised control" over vehicle within meaning of automatic stay statute by refusing to return vehicle to bankruptcy estate upon request; abrogating *In re Spears*, 223 B.R. 159. 11 U.S.C.A. § 362(a)(3).

Thompson v. General Motors Acceptance Corp., LLC, 566 F.3d 699, on remand In re Thompson, 426 B.R. 759.

Creditor's act of passively holding onto asset that was seized prepetition but belongs to bankruptcy estate constitutes "exercising control" over asset and violates automatic stay. 11 U.S.C.A. § 362(a)(3).

Thompson v. General Motors Acceptance Corp., LLC, 566 F.3d 699, on remand In re Thompson, 426 B.R. 759.

Debtor's right of possession of collateral is incident to automatic stay, and secured creditor's subjectively perceived lack of adequate protection is not exception to stay provision and does not defeat this right. 11 U.S.C.A. § 362(a).

Thompson v. General Motors Acceptance Corp., LLC, 566 F.3d 699, on remand In re Thompson, 426 B.R. 759.

Upon request of debtor that has filed for bankruptcy, creditor must first return asset in which debtor has interest to his bankruptcy estate and then, if necessary, seek adequate protection of its interests in bankruptcy court; abrogating *In re Nash*, 228 B.R. 669, and *In re Spears*, 223 B.R. 159. 11 U.S.C.A. §§ 363(e), 542(a).

Thompson v. General Motors Acceptance Corp., LLC, 566 F.3d 699, on remand In re Thompson, 426 B.R. 759.

C.A.6 (Mich.) 2012. Once a bankruptcy petition is filed, judgments cannot be enforced against the debtor, the debtor's property cannot be repossessed or foreclosed on, and liens cannot be perfected or enforced against the debtor's property. 11 U.S.C.A. § 362(a).

In re Global Technovations Inc., 694 F.3d 705.

M.D.Ga. 2003. Motor vehicle to which, under Georgia law, debtor continued to hold legal title even after it was repossessed by secured creditor four days before commencement of debtor's Chapter 13 case was included in "property of the estate," and was protected by automatic stay; thus, by refusing to turn vehicle over at debtor's request, creditor was in con-

tempt of automatic stay provision. Bankr.Code, 11 U.S.C.A. §§ 362, 541(a).

Motors Acceptance Corp. v. Rozier, 290 B.R. 910, question certified In re Rozier, 348 F.3d 1305, certified question answered 597 S.E.2d 367, 278 Ga. 52, answer to certified question conformed to 376 F.3d 1323, affirmed 376 F.3d 1323.

N.D.N.Y. 2012. Upon receiving notice of debtor's Chapter 13 filing, creditor was obligated to return, for use by reorganization estate, a motor vehicle which it had lawfully repossessed prepetition, but in which debtor still had redemptive rights; creditor's failure to return vehicle for nearly two months while waiting for debtor to file and prosecute a turnover motion was violation of automatic stay, as act to obtain possession of, or to exercise control over, property of the estate. 11 U.S.C.A. § 362(a)(3).

Weber v. SEFCU, 477 B.R. 308.

S.D.Tex. 2004. Once Chapter 13 debtor had made demand for return of motor vehicle which bank had lawfully repossessed prepetition and provided proof that vehicle was insured, bank could not retain vehicle based upon its unilateral determination that its security interest in vehicle was not adequately protected; bank's retention of motor vehicle, after two demands for turnover by debtor, was violation of automatic stay, as being in nature of act to "exercise control over property of the estate." Bankr.Code, 11 U.S.C.A. § 362(a)(3).

Mitchell v. BankIllinois, 316 B.R. 891.

8th Cir.BAP (Mo.) 2007. Local bankruptcy rule requiring debtors to maintain insurance coverage on vehicles serving as collateral and permitting secured creditors, prior to obtaining relief from the stay, to take possession of such vehicles pending presentation of proof of insurance, enlarged creditors' rights beyond the scope permitted by the automatic stay section of the Bankruptcy Code and the bankruptcy rule governing stay relief and, thus, was invalid; practical effect of local rule was to permit a creditor to obtain property of the estate or of the debtor through "instant self-help" without permission from the court and without even filing a motion, in derogation of the limited ex parte relief allowed under the bankruptcy rules. 11 U.S.C.A. § 362(a); Fed.Rules Bankr.Proc. Rule 4001(a), 11 U.S.C.A.; U.S.Bankr.Ct.Rules W.D.Mo., Rule 4070-1.D.

In re Suggs, 377 B.R. 198.

10th Cir.BAP (Wyo.) 2005. Creditor's retention, postpetition, of motor vehicle which it had lawfully repossessed from Chapter 13 debtors prior to commencement of their bankruptcy case constituted an "exercise of control" over property of the estate and violated automatic stay. 11 U.S.C.A. § 362(a)(3).

In re Yates, 332 B.R. 1.

† **This Case was not selected for publication in the National Reporter System**
For cited U.S.C.A. sections and legislative history, see United States Code Annotated

WEST'S
FEDERAL PRACTICE
DIGEST 4th

Volume 6B

BANKRUPTCY ⚷ 2398 to 2426

THOMSON
✳
™
WEST

Mat # 40411168

Bkrtcy.E.D.Va. 1999. While the Bankruptcy Code preserves right of setoff as it may exist prepetition, once bankruptcy petition is filed, creditor's right of setoff is subject to automatic stay. Bankr.Code, 11 U.S.C.A. § 362(a)(7).

In re Carlyle, 242 B.R. 881.

Bkrtcy.E.D.Va. 1995. Unlike recoupment, creditor's right of setoff is subject to automatic stay, and creditor's right of setoff is not recognized in bankruptcy unless both opposing claims arose before petition date, whereas recoupment is not so limited, for it may be invoked where creditor's claim arose prepetition and debtor's claim postpetition. Bankr.Code, 11 U.S.C.A. §§ 362(a)(7), 553(a).

In re Thompson, 182 B.R. 140, subsequently affirmed 92 F.3d 1182.

Disability and retirement plan administered by county police officers retirement system was contract, not government-entitlement program, for purposes of determining whether doctrine of recoupment, as "equitable exception" to automatic stay, applied to allow retirement system's board of trustees to withhold benefits payable to Chapter 7 debtor in order to recover overpayments made to him in prior years; although plan was creation of statute, plan was part of overall compensation and retirement package made available to police department employees, and not to general populace simply on basis of demonstrated need. Bankr.Code, 11 U.S.C.A. § 362; Va.Code 1950, § 51.1–805, subd. 2; § 51–127.26 (Repealed).

In re Thompson, 182 B.R. 140, subsequently affirmed 92 F.3d 1182.

Equity alone cannot invoke recoupment; instead, countervailing demands at issue must arise from same transaction in order for creditor to use recoupment to avoid automatic stay. Bankr.Code, 11 U.S.C.A. § 362.

In re Thompson, 182 B.R. 140, subsequently affirmed 92 F.3d 1182.

Bkrtcy.E.D.Va. 1985. Automatic stay prohibits exercise of right of setoff, but does not destroy right to setoff itself. Bankr.Code, 11 U.S.C.A. §§ 362, 553.

In re Conti, 50 B.R. 142.

Bkrtcy.E.D.Wis. 1991. Creditor is prohibited from applying setoff rights under bankruptcy statute unless relief from automatic stay is granted. Bank.Code, 11 U.S.C.A. §§ 362(a)(7), 553.

In re Express Freight Lines, Inc., 130 B.R. 288.

⟳2400. —— Repossession.

C.A.9 (Cal.) 1987. Automatic stay in the Bankruptcy Code applied to Chapter 11 debtor's appeal of deficiency judgment obtained by creditor who sold repossessed collateral. Bankr. Code, 11 U.S.C.A. §§ 362(a), 1101 et seq.

Ingersoll-Rand Financial Corp. v. Miller Min. Co., Inc., 817 F.2d 1424.

C.A.11 (Ga.) 2004. Where, under Georgia law, legal title and right of redemption remained with Chapter 13 debtor even after secured creditor had lawfully repossessed motor vehicle securing its claim prepetition, motor vehicle was included in "property of the estate" and was protected by automatic stay; on petition date, creditor had not yet complied with disposition or retention procedures of the Georgia Uniform Commercial Code (U.C.C.). Bankr.Code, 11 U.S.C.A. §§ 362(a), 541(a); West's Ga.Code Ann. § 11-9-101 et seq.

In re Rozier, 376 F.3d 1323.

C.A.11 (Ga.) 2003. To extent that, following creditor's repossession of motor vehicle securing its claim, both legal title to vehicle and right of redemption remained with debtor under governing Georgia law, vehicle was included in "property of the estate" when debtor later filed for Chapter 13 relief, and was protected by automatic stay. Bankr.Code, 11 U.S.C.A. §§ 362, 541(a)(1).

In re Rozier, 348 F.3d 1305, certified question answered Motors Acceptance Corp. v. Rozier, 597 S.E.2d 367, 278 Ga. 52, answer to certified question conformed to 376 F.3d 1323.

To extent that, following creditor's repossession of motor vehicle securing its claim, legal title passed to creditor under governing Georgia law and debtor retained only a right of redemption, vehicle was not included in "property of the estate" when debtor later filed for Chapter 13 relief, and was not protected by automatic stay. Bankr.Code, 11 U.S.C.A. §§ 362, 541(a)(1).

In re Rozier, 348 F.3d 1305, certified question answered Motors Acceptance Corp. v. Rozier, 597 S.E.2d 367, 278 Ga. 52, answer to certified question conformed to 376 F.3d 1323.

N.D.Ala. 1997. Automobile that secured creditor had repossessed, based on debtors' default, after prior Chapter 13 case was dismissed and before debtors could again file for Chapter 13 relief, was not included in property of second Chapter 13 estate, such that creditor's failure to turn car over to Chapter 13 trustee did not violate automatic stay; at time second Chapter 13 petition was filed, debtor no longer had title to car under Alabama law, and had right to redeem it only by making full payment of debt secured by car and creditor's reasonable ex-

† This Case was not selected for publication in the National Reporter System
For cited U.S.C.A. sections and legislative history, see United States Code Annotated

14

WEST'S
BANKRUPTCY
DIGEST

Volume 5B

BANKRUPTCY  2397 to 2420

WEST.
A Thomson Reuters business

Mat # 41012571

Law Rev. 2010. The Bankruptcy Code Without Safe Harbors. Stephen J. Lubben.
84 Am. Bankr. L.J. 123.

Law Rev. 2008. Processing Credit Card Charges in Chapter 11. Gary W. Marsh, David E. Gordon.
82 Am. Bankr. L.J. 253.

Law Rev. 2006. Repurchase Obligations Under Mortgage Loan Sale Agreements - Protection from the Automatic Stay and Future Avoidance Actions. Bruce H. White, William L. Medford and Bryan L. Elwood.
25 SEP Am. Bankr. Inst. J. 40.

⊸**2400. —— Repossession.**

C.A.9 (Cal.) 1987. Automatic stay in the Bankruptcy Code applied to Chapter 11 debtor's appeal of deficiency judgment obtained by creditor who sold repossessed collateral. Bankr.Code, 11 U.S.C.A. §§ 362(a), 1101 et seq.
Ingersoll-Rand Financial Corp. v. Miller Min. Co., Inc., 817 F.2d 1424.

C.A.11 (Ga.) 2004. Where, under Georgia law, legal title and right of redemption remained with Chapter 13 debtor even after secured creditor had lawfully repossessed motor vehicle securing its claim prepetition, motor vehicle was included in "property of the estate" and was protected by automatic stay; on petition date, creditor had not yet complied with disposition or retention procedures of the Georgia Uniform Commercial Code (U.C.C.). Bankr.Code, 11 U.S.C.A. §§ 362(a), 541(a); West's Ga.Code Ann. § 11-9-101 et seq.
In re Rozier, 376 F.3d 1323.

C.A.11 (Ga.) 2003. To extent that, following creditor's repossession of motor vehicle securing its claim, both legal title to vehicle and right of redemption remained with debtor under governing Georgia law, vehicle was included in "property of the estate" when debtor later filed for Chapter 13 relief, and was protected by automatic stay. Bankr.Code, 11 U.S.C.A. §§ 362, 541(a)(1).
In re Rozier, 348 F.3d 1305, certified question answered Motors Acceptance Corp. v. Rozier, 597 S.E.2d 367, 278 Ga. 52, answer to certified question conformed to 376 F.3d 1323.

To extent that, following creditor's repossession of motor vehicle securing its claim, legal title passed to creditor under governing Georgia law and debtor retained only a right of redemption, vehicle was not included in "property of the estate" when debtor later filed for Chapter 13 relief, and was not protected by automatic stay. Bankr.Code, 11 U.S.C.A. §§ 362, 541(a)(1).
In re Rozier, 348 F.3d 1305, certified question answered Motors Acceptance Corp. v. Rozier, 597 S.E.2d 367, 278 Ga. 52, answer to certified question conformed to 376 F.3d 1323.

C.A.7 (Ill.) 2009. Secured creditor that had repossessed Chapter 13 debtor's vehicle prepetition "exercised control" over vehicle within meaning of automatic stay statute by refusing to return vehicle to bankruptcy estate upon request; abrogating In re Spears, 223 B.R. 159. 11 U.S.C.A. § 362(a)(3).
Thompson v. General Motors Acceptance Corp., LLC, 566 F.3d 699, on remand In re Thompson, 426 B.R. 759.

Creditor's act of passively holding onto asset that was seized prepetition but belongs to bankruptcy estate constitutes "exercising control" over asset and violates automatic stay. 11 U.S.C.A. § 362(a)(3).
Thompson v. General Motors Acceptance Corp., LLC, 566 F.3d 699, on remand In re Thompson, 426 B.R. 759.

Debtor's right of possession of collateral is incident to automatic stay, and secured creditor's subjectively perceived lack of adequate protection is not exception to stay provision and does not defeat this right. 11 U.S.C.A. § 362(a).
Thompson v. General Motors Acceptance Corp., LLC, 566 F.3d 699, on remand In re Thompson, 426 B.R. 759.

Upon request of debtor that has filed for bankruptcy, creditor must first return asset in which debtor has interest to his bankruptcy estate and then, if necessary, seek adequate protection of its interests in bankruptcy court; abrogating In re Nash,

TWELFTH DECENNIAL DIGEST

Part 2

AMERICAN DIGEST SYSTEM

2010 – 2013

*A Complete Digest of All Decisions of the State and
Federal Courts as Reported in the National
Reporter System and the State Reports*

Volume 7

BANKRUPTCY ☞ 2391 to 3500

 THOMSON REUTERS™

Mat # 41357499

Bankruptcy court has some discretion in determining whether party's contract with debtor is deserving of special protections reserved for forward contracts. 11 U.S.C.A. § 101(25), 362(b)(6), 546(e), 548(d)(2)(B), 556.—Id.

While Chapter 11 debtor, as entity that had entered into contract with electric power company to supply company with electricity at specific cost from solar generating facility that it would construct, was arguably itself a "forward contract merchant," electric power company, as entity that, for hedging purposes, regularly entered into contracts with short- and long-term maturity dates for future delivery of electricity, qualified as "forward contract merchant," which was sufficient, regardless of debtor's possible status as such a merchant, to bring company's exercise of contractual rights granted to it under its forward contract with debtor within terms of stay exception. 11 U.S.C.A. §§ 101(26), 362(b)(6).—Id.

As part of process of terminating its forward contract with Chapter 11 debtor or of exercise of its security interest in cash or cash equivalents that debtor had posted to secure its contractual obligations, both of which were excepted from automatic stay, electric power company was entitled to set off or net out certain payments or obligations against security that debtor had posted. 11 U.S.C.A. §§ 362(b)(6), 556.—Id.

Bkrtcy.D.Del. 2012. Creditors seeking to exercise right of setoff in bankruptcy cannot do so unilaterally, without first obtaining relief from automatic stay. 11 U.S.C.A. §§ 362(d), 553.— In re WL Homes LLC, 471 B.R. 349.

Bkrtcy.N.D.Ga. 2011. While commencement of bankruptcy case stays the exercise of right of setoff against property of debtor, setoff provision of the Bankruptcy Code specifies that no provision other than that imposing stay, including preference and fraudulent transfer provisions, may be used to avoid or otherwise destroy the limited setoff rights preserved by setoff provision. 11 U.S.C.A. §§ 362(a), 547, 548, 553(a).—In re MCB Financial Group, Inc., 461 B.R. 914.

Bkrtcy.C.D.Ill. 2011. Exercise of recoupment rights does not violate automatic stay. 11 U.S.C.A. § 362(a).—In re Prochnow, 474 B.R. 607, affirmed 467 B.R. 656.

Creditor's exercise of setoff rights in bankruptcy requires relief from automatic stay. 11 U.S.C.A. § 362(d), 553.—Id.

While real estate brokerage firm which employed Chapter 7 debtor could not exercise right of setoff, to reduce/eliminate its obligation to debtor for commissions earned prepetition based on debtor's prepetition obligation to reimburse it for certain expenses, without first moving for relief from automatic stay, firm's placement of temporary freeze on commissions until stay relief could be obtained did not violate automatic stay. 11 U.S.C.A. § 362(a).—Id.

Bkrtcy.N.D.Ill. 2012. While Bankruptcy Code preserves right of setoff, no postpetition setoff is permissible without relief from automatic stay. 11 U.S.C.A. § 362(a)(7), 553.—In re Quade, 482 B.R. 217.

Bkrtcy.S.D.N.Y. 2011. "Safe harbor" exceptions to automatic stay, that provide for exercise of contractual right of setoff in connection with swap agreements notwithstanding the operation of any provision of the Bankruptcy Code which could operate to "stay, avoid or otherwise limit" that right, could not be interpreted as implicitly, and without specific reference to setoff provision of the Code, doing away with mutuality requirement for exercise of right of setoff in bankruptcy; to require that offsetting balances be mutual did not stay, avoid or limit any setoff rights that creditor possessed under alleged swap agreement with debtor, inasmuch as creditor had no right of setoff in bankruptcy, of kind which could be

stayed, avoided or limited, unless requisite mutuality existed in first place. 11 U.S.C.A. §§ 553, 561.—In re Lehman Bros. Inc., 458 B.R. 134.

Creditor's good faith belief that triangular right of setoff expressly permitted under its prepetition swap agreement with Chapter 11 debtor, in combination with "safe harbor" exceptions to automatic stay, enabled it to unilaterally set off prepetition debts that were owed, not by debtor, but by its affiliated entities, did not excuse stay violation that occurred when creditor, without moving for relief from stay, exercised control over property of estate by retaining funds in exercise of its alleged triangular setoff rights. 11 U.S.C.A. §§ 362(a), 553, 561.—Id.

Bkrtcy.S.D.N.Y. 2010. Collateral in Chapter 11 debtor's cash collateral account with bank had no direct or indirect relationship to claims of bank against debtor arising under swap agreement and was pledged by debtor exclusively to secure overdraft risks, and therefore exception to automatic stay addressing contractual netting rights under swap agreements did not apply to bank's postpetition setoff using funds in cash collateral account to offset unrelated swap exposure. 11 U.S.C.A. § 362(b)(17).—In re Lehman Bros. Holdings Inc., 439 B.R. 811.

Bkrtcy.S.D.N.Y. 2010. "Safe harbor" exceptions to automatic stay, that provide for exercise of contractual right of offset in connection with swap agreements notwithstanding the operation of any provision of the Bankruptcy Code that could operate to stay, avoid or otherwise limit that right, could not be interpreted as implicitly, and without specific reference to setoff provision of the Code, doing away with one of the bedrock requirements for exercise of right of setoff in bankruptcy, i.e., that debts and claims be mutual; to require that offsetting balances be mutual did not stay, avoid or limit any setoff rights that creditor possessed under alleged swap agreement with Chapter 11 debtor, inasmuch as creditor had no right of setoff in bankruptcy, of kind which could be stayed, avoided or limited, unless requisite mutuality existed in first place. 11 U.S.C.A. §§ 553(a), 560(a), 561(a).—In re Lehman Bros. Holdings, Inc., 433 B.R. 101, affirmed 445 B.R. 130.

"Safe harbor" exceptions to automatic stay, that provide for exercise of contractual right of offset in connection with swap agreements notwithstanding the operation of any provision of the Bankruptcy Code which could operate to stay, avoid or otherwise limit that right, are intended to permit parties to swap agreements to exercise right to offset or net termination values, despite the automatic stay and without having to seek relief from stay. 11 U.S.C.A. §§ 362, 560(a), 561(a).—Id.

Bkrtcy.E.D.Pa. 2012. Counterclaims asserted by defendants against Chapter 11 debtor in debtor's adversary proceeding were subject to the automatic stay. 11 U.S.C.A. § 362(a).—In re Drauschak, 481 B.R. 330.

Bkrtcy.D.Puerto Rico 2010. Claims asserted by claimants in arbitration proceedings before the Financial Industry Regulatory Authority (FINRA) involving Chapter 11 debtor's duly dissolved subsidiary, a nondebtor, did not fall within the exception to the automatic stay for the exercise of certain contractual rights under security agreements or arrangements; the relevant section of the Bankruptcy Code allowed for setoffs, which involve mutual debts and claims, which in turn originate from short-term contracts, such as securities and commodities contracts which involve margin calls, and entered into by certain entities described in said section, while the FINRA claimants' causes of actions arose from alleged violations of securities laws which occurred with respect to the subsidiary before it was liquidated.

11 U.S.C.A. § 362(b)(6).—In re R & G Financial Corp., 441 B.R. 401.

Bkrtcy.D.S.C. 2012. Automatic stay does not apply to recoupment of obligations which arise out of same transaction, nor is recoupment prohibited by discharge injunction. 11 U.S.C.A. §§ 362(a), 524(a).—In re Fischbach, 464 B.R. 258.

☜2400. —— Repossession.

C.A.6 (Mich.) 2012. Once a bankruptcy petition is filed, judgments cannot be enforced against the debtor, the debtor's property cannot be repossessed or foreclosed on, and liens cannot be perfected or enforced against the debtor's property. 11 U.S.C.A. § 362(a).—In re Global Technovations Inc., 694 F.3d 705.

N.D.Ala. 2013. Creditor who wrongfully repossesses debtor's property postpetition has affirmative obligation to restore situation to the status quo, and creditor's failure to do so constitutes a continuing violation of automatic stay. 11 U.S.C.A. § 362(a).—Credit Nation Lending Services, LLC v. Nettles, 489 B.R. 239.

Creditor that wrongfully repossessed Chapter 13 debtors' motor vehicle postpetition in willful violation of automatic stay, merely by making vehicle available for debtors to pick up at location in adjoining state, did not restore situation to status quo ante, as it existed on petition date, and its refusal to do more to remedy its stay violation was in nature of continuing violation of automatic stay. 11 U.S.C.A. § 362(a).—Id.

N.D.N.Y. 2012. Upon receiving notice of debtor's Chapter 13 filing, creditor was obligated to return, for use by reorganization estate, a motor vehicle which it had lawfully repossessed prepetition, but in which debtor still had redemptive rights; creditor's failure to return vehicle for nearly two months while waiting for debtor to file and prosecute a turnover motion was violation of automatic stay, as act to obtain possession of, or to exercise control over, property of the estate. 11 U.S.C.A. § 362(a)(3).—Weber v. SEFCU, 477 B.R. 308, affirmed In re Weber, 719 F.3d 72.

Bkrtcy.S.D.Cal. 2010. Chapter 13 debtor's vehicle remained property of bankruptcy estate after termination of automatic stay against debtor, based upon pendency and dismissal of debtor's prior bankruptcy case in preceding year, such that stay remained in force and effect as to vehicle and creditor's repossession of vehicle violated stay. 11 U.S.C.A. § 362(c)(3)(A).—In re Alvarez, 432 B.R. 839.

Bkrtcy.E.D.Mich. 2012. Creditor's conduct, upon learning that it would have to return to Chapter 13 debtor a motor vehicle that it had lawfully repossessed prepetition, in disabling vehicle's ignition system so that debtor could not start vehicle, was violation of automatic stay, as act to exercise control over property of the estate and to recover from debtor on claim that arose prepetition. 11 U.S.C.A. § 362(a)(3, 6).—In re Mabone, 471 B.R. 534.

Bkrtcy.S.D.Miss. 2012. Creditor's refusal to turn over Chapter 13 debtor's vehicle, which it had repossessed prepetition pursuant to Mississippi Title Pledge Act, did not violate automatic stay where debtor's unexpired right to redeem vehicle, but not vehicle itself, was estate property. 11 U.S.C.A. §§ 362, 541(a)(1); West's A.M.C. § 75–67–411(4).—In re Bolton, 466 B.R. 831.

Bkrtcy.S.D.N.Y. 2012. Creditor had duty to turn over motor vehicle that it had repossessed prepetition to Chapter 7 debtors upon the filing of their bankruptcy petition, and by failing to do so and insisting, as condition to return of vehicle, that debtor first pay any arrears and execute reaffirmation agreement, it violated automatic

† This Case was not selected for publication in the National Reporter System
For Later Case History Information, see KeyCite on WESTLAW

18

WEST'S
CALIFORNIA DIGEST 2d

Volume 5B

BAIL — BANKRUPTCY 2670

ST. PAUL, MINN.

WEST GROUP

right to liquidate stocks securing debtor's loan to cover margin calls pursuant to automatic stay exception for certain stockbroker setoffs, in that agreement obligated stockbroker to deal with debtor's loan and collateral in accordance with its terms, and thus gave rise to potential claim against stockbroker which, although unmatured at time of filing, fell within Bankruptcy Code's broad definition of "debt" for setoff purposes. Bankr.Code, 11 U.S.C.A. §§ 101(5, 12), 362(b)(6).

    In re Weisberg, 136 F.3d 655, certiorari denied Wolkowitz v. Shearson Lehman Bros., Inc., 119 S.Ct. 72, 525 U.S. 826, 142 L.Ed.2d 56.

Client agreement between debtor and stockbroker that authorized stockbroker to sell debtor's stocks in the event debtor failed to meet margin call was properly deemed to be "securities contract" for purposes of stockbroker's right to perform certain setoffs under automatic stay exception; that stocks in debtor's margin account were pledged as collateral for loan was irrelevant. Bankr.Code, 11 U.S.C.A. § 362(b)(6).

    In re Weisberg, 136 F.3d 655, certiorari denied Wolkowitz v. Shearson Lehman Bros., Inc., 119 S.Ct. 72, 525 U.S. 826, 142 L.Ed.2d 56.

N.D.Cal. 1998. United States Health and Human Services Department's (HHS) prepetition Medicare overpayments to debtor-nursing home were logically related to HHS's postpetition underpayment obligations to debtor, and, thus, were part of single transaction for equitable reimbursement purposes, even though overpayments and underpayments did not occur in same fiscal year; thus, HHS could obtain reimbursement for prepetition overpayments by setting-off postpetition underpayments without violating automatic stay. Bankr.Code, 11 U.S.C.A. § 362(a); Social Security Act, § 1801(a), as amended, 42 U.S.C.A. § 1395g(a); 42 C.F.R. § 405.370.

    Sims v. U.S. Dept. of Human Services, 225 B.R. 709, affirmed In re TLC Hospitals, Inc., 224 F.3d 1008.

9th Cir.BAP (Cal.) 1996. Stockbroker-creditor's postpetition liquidations of stock, which Chapter 11 debtor pledged as security for $50,000 loan from creditor, in order to satisfy margin maintenance calls came within automatic stay exception allowing stockbroker or financial institution to set off claim for margin payment with securities of debtor that broker holds to margin, secure, or settle securities contract, though trustee claimed that transaction involved only loan and pledge of stock as collater-

al; pledge was "sale" of stock. Bankr.Code, 11 U.S.C.A. § 362(b)(6).

    In re Weisberg, 193 B.R. 916, affirmed in part, reversed in part 136 F.3d 655, certiorari denied Wolkowitz v. Shearson Lehman Bros., Inc., 119 S.Ct. 72, 525 U.S. 826, 142 L.Ed.2d 56.

Stockbroker or financial institution is not stayed from exercising its right to set off claim for margin payment with securities of debtor that broker holds to margin, secure, or settle securities contract. Bankr.Code, 11 U.S.C.A. § 362(b)(6).

    In re Weisberg, 193 B.R. 916, affirmed in part, reversed in part 136 F.3d 655, certiorari denied Wolkowitz v. Shearson Lehman Bros., Inc., 119 S.Ct. 72, 525 U.S. 826, 142 L.Ed.2d 56.

9th Cir.BAP (Cal.) 1988. Automatic stay does not defeat right of setoff, but rather, merely stays its enforcement pending orderly examination of debtor's and creditor's rights. Bankr. Code, 11 U.S.C.A. §§ 362(a)(7), 553.

    In re Pieri, 86 B.R. 208.

Bkrtcy.C.D.Cal. 1999. Internal Revenue Service's (IRS's) postpetition setoff of tax overpayment owing to Chapter 7 debtor-taxpayer against debtor's prepetition debt for unpaid taxes in prior year violated automatic stay. Bankr. Code, 11 U.S.C.A. § 362(a).

    In re Schield, 242 B.R. 1.

Bkrtcy.S.D.Cal. 1996. Creditor does not have to obtain relief from automatic stay for recoupment.

    In re Heffernan Memorial Hosp. Dist., 192 B.R. 228.

Bkrtcy.S.D.Cal. 1980. Creditor that did not exercise setoff prior to Chapter 11 petition being filed had to obtain relief from automatic stay. Bankr.Code, 11 U.S.C.A. § 362(a)(7).

    In re Princess Baking Corp., 5 B.R. 587.

☞2400. ——— Repossession.

C.A.9 (Cal.) 1987. Automatic stay in the Bankruptcy Code applied to Chapter 11 debtor's appeal of deficiency judgment obtained by creditor who sold repossessed collateral. Bankr. Code, 11 U.S.C.A. §§ 362(a), 1101 et seq.

    Ingersoll-Rand Financial Corp. v. Miller Min. Co., Inc., 817 F.2d 1424.

9th Cir.BAP (Cal.) 1983. Fact that seller of propane tank had contract right to repossess upon default did not entitle it to repossess tank in violation of automatic stay. Bankr.Code, 11 U.S.C.A. § 362(a)(3).

    In re Zartun, 30 B.R. 543.

Bkrtcy.S.D.Cal. 1998. Secured creditor's postpetition repossession of debtor's automobile violates automatic stay, is void and of no effect,

West's
FEDERAL PRACTICE
DIGEST 5th

Vol. 38

Bankruptcy ⚷ 2341 to 2420

2013
Cumulative Annual Pocket Part
Covering opinions 2013 to date

THE WEST DIGEST TOPIC NUMBERS WHICH CAN BE
USED FOR WESTLAW® SEARCHES ARE LISTED ON
PAGE III OF THIS POCKET PART.

All Federal Case Law of
The Modern Era

**Up-Dated Weekly by West's Reporter Advance Sheets
or WESTLAW**

**For Prior Cases Consult Federal Digest,
Modern Federal Practice Digest,
Federal Practice Digest 2d and Federal
Practice Digest 3d**

 THOMSON REUTERS™

that debtor comply with trial subpoena previously served upon him and appear at trial to give testimony against his alleged co-conspirators, especially where individual and individual's attorneys did not ultimately call debtor as witness in state court conspiracy action, did not require debtor to produce any documents, and relied on evidence derived entirely from other sources to prove their case against co-conspirators. 11 U.S.C.A. § 362(a)(1).—Id.

Chapter 7 debtor's conduct, as alleged participant in conspiracy to fraudulently transfer assets, was plainly relevant to claims asserted in state court lawsuit against his alleged co-conspirators, and state court plaintiff's elicitation of testimony regarding debtor's conduct in support of claims that ultimately resulted in issuance of jury verdict for more than $3 million against his alleged co-conspirators did not violate automatic stay, as alleged attempt to recover on prepetition claim against debtor, not even if this testimony might support future liability claims against debtor, and not even if state court plaintiff referred to this testimony in support of nondischargeability proceeding commenced in debtor's bankruptcy case. 11 U.S.C.A. § 362(a)(6).—Id.

⟋2396. —— Co-debtors and third persons.
S.D.N.Y. 2013. Automatic stay generally protects only the debtor, property of the debtor, or property of the estate; it does not protect non-debtor parties or their property. 11 U.S.C.A. § 362(a).—Securities Investor Protection Corp. v. Bernard L. Madoff Investment Securities LLC, 490 B.R. 59.

Independent third-party claims against non-debtor parties generally are not subject to the automatic stay. 11 U.S.C.A. § 362(a)(1).—Id.

Where a non-debtor's liability rests upon his own breach of duty, a stay cannot be extended to the non-debtor, even where the debtor and non-debtors are joint tortfeasors. 11 U.S.C.A. § 362(a)(1).—Id.

⟋2397(1). In general.
Bkrtcy.W.D.Ky. 2013. While the discharge in debtor's first Chapter 7 case enjoined debtor's in personam liability for his mortgage debt, which was secured by an unrecorded mortgage, once the case was closed mortgagee was free to record the mortgage and pursue in rem foreclosure of the subject property under Kentucky law, and trustee in debtor's second Chapter 7 case could not avoid the mortgage; the unrecorded mortgage was not avoided in debtor's first case, mortgagee's right to foreclose on mortgage in rem passed through first case unaffected, upon trustee's abandonment of the property title to it revested in debtor subject to debtor's contractual mortgage lien, and mortgagee's subsequent recording of the mortgage was neither prohibited by the automatic stay nor violative of the discharge injunction, but served to preserve mortgagee's right to its contractual liquidation preference from the proceeds of the property. 11 U.S.C.A. §§ 362(c)(2)(C), 524(a), 544(a)(3).—In re Williams, 490 B.R. 236.

⟋2397(2). Foreclosure proceedings.
Bkrtcy.E.D.Tex. 2013. Automatic stay protected Chapter 7 debtor from creditor's efforts to evict her from her home, even though creditor had foreclosed on the home prepetition such that the home was not property of the estate. 11 U.S.C.A. § 362(a).—In re Nevarez, 488 B.R. 332.

⟋2399. —— Set-offs and counterclaims; cross claims.
Bkrtcy.D.Ariz. 2013. Ordinary supply contracts should not receive the special protections accorded in bankruptcy to forward contracts; ordinary supply contract is not "forward contract." 11 U.S.C.A. § 101(25), 362(b)(6), 546(e), 548(d)(2)(B), 556.—In re Clear Peak Energy, Inc., 488 B.R. 647.

In according special treatment in bankruptcy to forward contracts, Congress generally sought to protect financial markets from instability that bankruptcy proceedings might cause. 11 U.S.C.A. § 101(25), 362(b)(6), 546(e), 548(d)(2)(B), 556.—Id.

Bankruptcy court has some discretion in determining whether party's contract with debtor is deserving of special protections reserved for forward contracts. 11 U.S.C.A. § 101(25), 362(b)(6), 546(e), 548(d)(2)(B), 556.—Id.

While Chapter 11 debtor, as entity that had entered into contract with electric power company to supply company with electricity at specific cost from solar generating facility that it would construct, was arguably itself a "forward contract merchant," electric power company, as entity that, for hedging purposes, regularly entered into contracts with short- and long-term maturity dates for future delivery of electricity, qualified as "forward contract merchant," which was sufficient, regardless of debtor's possible status as such a merchant, to bring company's exercise of contractual rights granted to it under its forward contract with debtor within terms of stay exception. 11 U.S.C.A. §§ 101(26), 362(b)(6).—Id.

As part of process of terminating its forward contract with Chapter 11 debtor or of exercise of its security interest in cash or cash equivalents that debtor had posted to secure its contractual obligations, both of which were excepted from automatic stay, electric power company was entitled to set off or net out certain payments or obligations against security that debtor had posted. 11 U.S.C.A. §§ 362(b)(6), 556.—Id.

⟋2400. —— Repossession.
N.D.Ala. 2013. Creditor who wrongfully repossesses debtor's property postpetition has affirmative obligation to restore situation to the status quo, and creditor's failure to do so constitutes a continuing violation of automatic stay. 11 U.S.C.A. § 362(a).—Credit Nation Lending Services, LLC v. Nettles, 489 B.R. 239.

Creditor that wrongfully repossessed Chapter 13 debtors' motor vehicle postpetition in willful violation of automatic stay, merely by making vehicle available for debtors to pick up at location in adjoining state, did not restore situation to status quo ante, as it existed on petition date, and its refusal to do more to remedy its stay violation was in nature of continuing violation of automatic stay. 11 U.S.C.A. § 362(a).—Id.

⟋2401. —— Domestic relations claims and proceedings.
† C.A.6 (Mich.) 2012. State-court attorney fee awards against Chapter 7 debtor, which arose from fees incurred by mother of debtor's children during custody dispute, amounted to "support" of children's parent under Bankruptcy Code's definition of domestic support obligation, as required for exception to automatic stay to apply and for resulting debt to be excepted from discharge; in issuing fee awards, state court looked at relative capacities of debtor and mother to pay fees, and reasoned that such awards could be necessary to enable party to prosecute or defend

† This Case was not selected for publication in the National Reporter System

American Jurisprudence 2d is a legal encyclopedia, containing an A-to-Z discussion of American law

Problem

A man goes to a party and has several beers. He gets into his car to drive home, but he realizes that the alcohol has affected him, so he pulls off the road into a highway rest area and decides to take a nap to help him feel more alert. He parks his car and turns off the engine, leaving the keys in the ignition. He quickly falls asleep. He is awakened by a flashlight shining in his eyes, and a police officer knocks on the window. He is given a breathalyzer test and fails it, and he is charged with driving while intoxicated, even though his car was parked and he was asleep. Find cases discussing what constitutes driving, operating, or being in physical control of a vehicle for purposes of a charge of driving while intoxicated.

Worksheet

Parties:

Places and Things:

Basis of Action or Issue:

Defense:

Relief Sought:

~Americvan Jurisprudence

SECOND EDITION

A MODERN COMPREHENSIVE TEXT STATEMENT
OF AMERICAN LAW

STATE AND FEDERAL

COMPLETELY REVISED AND REWRITTEN
IN THE LIGHT OF MODERN AUTHORITIES AND DEVELOPMENTS
BY THE EDITORIAL STAFF OF THE PUBLISHERS

GENERAL INDEX

2013 EDITION

A

The Index to American Jurisprudence 2d provides detailed coverage of all the articles in American Jurisprudence 2d so you can locate the information you need.

 THOMSON REUTERS™

Mat # 41262802

The American Jurisprudence 2d General Index indicates where there is a discussion of drinking alcoholic beverages in motor vehicles.The discussion is in Autos § 339. "Autos" is the abbreviation used for the Automobiles and Highway Traffic article.

Consult Correlation Tables in text volumes for references to materials published after this index

AMERICAN JURISPRUDENCE

SECOND EDITION

A MODERN COMPREHENSIVE TEXT STATEMENT OF
AMERICAN LAW

STATE AND FEDERAL

COMPLETELY REVISED AND REWRITTEN
IN THE LIGHT OF MODERN AUTHORITIES AND DEVELOPMENTS

Volume 7A

**AUTOMOBILE INSURANCE §§ 314 to 641
to
AUTOMOBILES AND HIGHWAY TRAFFIC §§ 1 to 401**

2007

This is the volume which contains section 339 of the Automobiles and Highway Traffic article.

THOMSON

WEST

For Customer Assistance Call 1-800-328-4880

Mat #40501519

§ 339 What constitutes "driving," "operating," or "being in actual physical control of" motor vehicle

Research References

West's Key Number Digest, Automobiles ⟜332
What constitutes driving, operating, or being in control of motor vehicle for purposes of driving while intoxicated statutes, 93 A.L.R.3d 7

While a defendant may be found guilty of the offense of driving under the influence on a showing of actual driving under the influence,[1] pursuant to various statutory provisions prescribing the offense, it is not necessary for an eyewitness to show that the defendant was driving the vehicle, so long as the defendant was in actual physical control.[2] The phrase "actual physical control" permits the apprehension of intoxicated prospective drivers before they place themselves and others at risk by driving; this aspect of the statute is a prophylactic measure that is intended to discourage intoxicated persons from entering motor vehicles except as passengers.[3]

However, a showing of "actual physical control" may require a showing that the motor was running and some evidence of the vehicle having been driven.[4] It is not necessary to show that the vehicle was in motion,[5] or that the motorist had the intent to put the car in motion.[6] However, in some jurisdictions, it is not sufficient to show that an intoxicated person started a parked car,[7] while in others the person may in fact be guilty although asleep in the vehicle.[8]

Whether or not a defendant was in actual physical control of a vehicle is a question for the fact finder based on the totality of the circumstances.[9] A court should look to whether the defendant actually posed a threat to the public by the exercise of present or imminent

---

[Section 339]

[1]Hughes v. State, 943 So. 2d 176 (Fla. Dist. Ct. App. 3d Dist. 2006), review denied (Fla. June 4, 2007).

[2]Cloyd v. State, 943 So. 2d 149 (Fla. Dist. Ct. App. 3d Dist. 2006), review denied (Fla. June 4, 2007); Com. v. Young, 2006 PA Super 193, 904 A.2d 947 (2006), appeal denied, 591 Pa. 664, 916 A.2d 633 (2006).

[3]State v. Adams, 142 Idaho 305, 127 P.3d 208 (Ct. App. 2005), review denied, (June 8, 2005).

[4]Com. v. Young, 2006 PA Super 193, 904 A.2d 947 (2006), appeal denied, 591 Pa. 664, 916 A.2d 633 (2006).

[5]Mezak v. State, 877 P.2d 1307 (Alaska Ct. App. 1994); State v. Larriva,

178 Ariz. 64, 870 P.2d 1160 (Ct. App. Div. 2 1993); Jenkins v. State, 223 Ga. App. 446, 478 S.E.2d 143 (1996); State v. Leopold, 179 Vt. 558, 889 A.2d 707 (2005).

[6]Russell v. State, 174 Ga. App. 436, 330 S.E.2d 175 (1985); People v. Scapes, 247 Ill. App. 3d 848, 187 Ill. Dec. 645, 617 N.E.2d 1366 (4th Dist. 1993); Garza v. State, 846 S.W.2d 936 (Tex. App. Houston 1st Dist. 1993), petition for discretionary review refused, (June 2, 1993).

[7]Com. v. Brotherson, 2005 PA Super 413, 888 A.2d 901 (2005), appeal denied, 587 Pa. 719, 899 A.2d 1121 (2006).

[8]Isom v. State, 105 Nev. 391, 776 P.2d 543 (1989).

[9]Barnett v. State, 671 So. 2d 135 (Ala. Crim. App. 1995); State v. Love, 182

control over the vehicle while impaired, rather than by simply using the vehicle as a stationary shelter,[10] but it may be sufficient to show a driver was in actual physical control even where a police officer finds a motorist slumped over in the passenger seat if the evidence indicates the person had been driving.[11] To determine whether the defendant is in actual physical control of a vehicle, the main factor is whether defendant is able to manipulate the vehicle's controls,[12] and it may be sufficient to show that the defendant has inserted the key into the ignition in order to roll up electronically operated windows.[13]

Courts are split relative to motorists sleeping with the engine off, some finding a driver to be in actual physical control of a vehicle where the driver is found sleeping in the car with the engine off,[14] while others deem that no actual physical control is exerted when the driver is found asleep in the driver's seat, with the engine off, and the key not in the ignition.[15] One does not "drive or operate" a car when there is a key in the ignition switch in the "off" position, as that does not engage the mechanical or electrical equipment of the car.[16]

Some courts may distinguish statutory provisions which prohibit operating a motor vehicle from those which prescribe driving while intoxicated.[17] In order to be "operating" a vehicle within the meaning of a statute proscribing driving while intoxicated, defendant must have exercised some control or manipulation over the vehicle, such as steering or backing or any physical handling of the controls for the purpose of putting the vehicle in motion.[18] Some courts have held that it is not necessary that the vehicle move,[19] while others require the

---

Ariz. 324, 897 P.2d 626 (1995).

[10]State v. Love, 182 Ariz. 324, 897 P.2d 626 (1995).

[11]State v. Ryan, 229 Mont. 7, 744 P.2d 1242 (1987) (engine running, feet near pedals, parked on a freeway on-ramp).

[12]Obrigewitch v. Director, North Dakota Dept. of Transp., 2002 ND 177, 653 N.W.2d 73 (N.D. 2002).

[13]State v. Kelton, 168 Vt. 629, 724 A.2d 452 (1998).

[14]People v. Davis, 205 Ill. App. 3d 431, 150 Ill. Dec. 349, 562 N.E.2d 1152 (1st Dist. 1990) (driver in back seat in sleeping bag, with keys in ignition and doors locked); Berns v. Commissioner of Public Safety, 355 N.W.2d 493 (Minn. Ct. App. 1984); City of Fargo v. Theusch, 462 N.W.2d 162 (N.D. 1990).

[15]State v. Fish, 228 Kan. 204, 612 P.2d 180 (1980).

[16]Stevenson v. City of Falls Church, 243 Va. 434, 416 S.E.2d 435 (1992).

[17]State v. Murray, 539 N.W.2d 368 (Iowa 1995); State v. Smith, 638 So. 2d 1212 (La. Ct. App. 1st Cir. 1994) (statute which prohibits "operating" a vehicle while intoxicated does not require proof that defendant was driving a vehicle); Milwaukee County v. Proegler, 95 Wis. 2d 614, 291 N.W.2d 608 (Ct. App. 1980) ("operate" has a meaning distinct from "drive" under the relevant statute).

[18]State v. Smith, 638 So. 2d 1212 (La. Ct. App. 1st Cir. 1994).

[19]State v. Murray, 539 N.W.2d 368 (Iowa 1995); State v. Smith, 638 So. 2d 1212 (La. Ct. App. 1st Cir. 1994).

vehicle to either be in motion or the engine running.[20] Some courts, however, simply say that to "operate" a vehicle under a statute prohibiting operating or attempting to operate a vehicle under the influence of alcohol means to drive it.[21]

Alternatively, once a person using a motor vehicle has put the vehicle in motion, or in a position posing a significant risk of causing a collision, such person continues to "operate" the vehicle until it is returned to a position posing no such risk.[22] In some jurisdictions, a running engine is not required to find that one was "operating" a vehicle.[23]

Some states have statutes which prohibit attempted operation of a motor vehicle while under the influence of alcohol or intoxicating liquor,[24] and in such cases the prosecution must prove beyond a reasonable doubt that the defendant intended to or did in fact operate the vehicle.[25]

§ 340 Places within proscription of statute

Research References

West's Key Number Digest, Automobiles ⟜332
Applicability, to operation of motor vehicle on private property, of legislation making drunken driving a criminal offense, 52 A.L.R.5th 655

With respect to the place where a statute proscribing the driving or operation of a motor vehicle while under the influence of intoxicants is applicable, the language of the statute generally controls.[1] Some statutes apply to drunken driving anywhere in the jurisdiction without providing that the offense must be committed on a public highway or in any other specified place,[2] and thus the offense may be committed

---

[20]Munson v. Iowa Dept. of Transp., Motor Vehicle Div., 513 N.W.2d 722 (Iowa 1994).

[21]State v. Kendall, 274 Kan. 1003, 58 P.3d 660 (2002).

[22]People v. Wood, 450 Mich. 399, 538 N.W.2d 351 (1995).

[23]State v. Mulcahy, 107 N.J. 467, 527 A.2d 368 (1987); State v. Gill, 70 Ohio St. 3d 150, 1994-Ohio-403, 637 N.E.2d 897 (1994).

[24]State v. Henderson, 416 A.2d 1261 (Me. 1980).

[25]State v. O'Malley, 120 N.H. 507, 416 A.2d 1387 (1980); People v. Dymond,

158 Misc. 2d 677, 601 N.Y.S.2d 1001 (County Ct. 1993).

[Section 340]

[1]Fitch v. State, 313 Ark. 122, 853 S.W.2d 874 (1993); State v. McGlone, 59 Ohio St. 3d 122, 570 N.E.2d 1115 (1991).

[2]Fitch v. State, 313 Ark. 122, 853 S.W.2d 874 (1993); People v. Bailey, 243 Ill. App. 3d 871, 184 Ill. Dec. 84, 612 N.E.2d 960 (5th Dist. 1993) (municipal parking lot fell within definition of "highway" where lot was publicly maintained and posted by municipality and was open to public); State v. McGlone, 59 Ohio St. 3d 122, 570 N.E.2d 1115 (1991).

American Law Reports articles summarize and discuss all U.S. state and federal case law on specific legal issues

Problem

Part of the experience of attending a baseball game is that many of the dozens of baseballs used in each game are hit out of play into foul territory, into the backstop and screens, and into the stands. When attendees are hit by a baseball and injured, they frequently charge that the stadium owner and/or baseball team should have provided more or better screens.

A child was struck in the head by a baseball during pregame batting practice at a minor league stadium while the child was seated in the picnic area beyond the unscreened left field wall in fair ball territory with his family for a pregame Little League party. The baseball club denied liability. Find the cases that address liability to a spectator at a baseball game who is hit by a ball due to the failure to provide or maintain sufficient screening at the picnic area of the baseball stadium.

Worksheet

Parties:

Places and Things:

Basis of Action or Issue:

Defense:

Relief Sought:

COVERING
ALR
ALR 2d
ALR 3d
ALR 4th
ALR 5th
ALR 6th, Vols. 1-35
ALR Federal
ALR Federal 2d, Vols. 1-30

The ALR Index is comprehensive to the entire ALR® series, where one can find all articles on a point of law.

Annotation History Table

INDEX

A-B

2008

Mat # 40756961

BARRICADES OR BARRIERS
—Cont'd
Construction contractor's liability for injuries to third persons by materials or debris on highway during course of construction or repair, **3 ALR4th 770, § 3, 5 to 13(a), 16 to 19, 22, 23, 25 to 27, 28(c), 29**

Curves, governmental duty to provide curve warnings or markings, **57 ALR4th 342, § 3 to 5(b), 6**

Eminent domain, damages resulting from temporary conditions incident to public improvements or repairs as compensable taking, **23 ALR4th 674, § 5, 6(b), 9**

Handicapped access, validity and construction of state statutes requiring construction of handicapped access facilities in buildings open to public, **82 ALR4th 121**

Pedestrians
  generally, **35 ALR4th 1117, § 11(b), 12**

  municipality, duty and liability of municipality as regards barriers for protection of adult pedestrians who may unintentionally deviate from street or highway into marginal or external hazards, **44 ALR2d 633**

Police chase, liability of governmental unit or its officers for injury to innocent occupant of moving vehicle or for damages to such vehicle as result of police chase, **4 ALR4th 865, § 4(a), 5(a)**

Repairs and maintenance, duty of operator of motor vehicle as affected by barrier placed to indicate that street is closed or undergoing repairs, **78 ALR 525**

Res ipsa loquitur, applicability of res ipsa loquitur in case of multiple, nonmedical defendants—modern status, **59 ALR4th 201, § 28**

Shoulder of street or highway, liability, in motor vehicle-related cases, of governmental entity for injury, death, or property damages resulting from defect or obstruction in shoulder of street or highway, **19 ALR4th 532, § 8, 10(a), 11, 12(b), 26, 35**

Trees, liability of governmental unit for injuries or damage resulting from tree or

BARRICADES OR BARRIERS
—Cont'd
limb falling onto highway from abutting land, **95 ALR3d 778, § 12(a)**

BARRIERS
Barricades or Barriers (this index)
Guardrails and Handrails (this index)

BARS AND TAVERNS
Taverns and Tavernkeepers (this index)

BARTER
Exchange of Property (this index)

BASEBALL
Adjoining property, liability of owner or operator of park or other premises on which baseball or other game is played, for injuries by ball to person on nearby street, sidewalk, or premises, **16 ALR2d 1458**

Antitrust, leagues or associations, application of state antitrust laws to athletic leagues or associations, **85 ALR3d 970**

Assault
  patron, liability of owner or operator of theater or other amusement to patron assaulted by another patron, **75 ALR3d 441, § 16**

  players, liability of participant in team athletic competition for injury to or death of another participant, **55 ALR5th 529, § 3(b)**

Auditoriums. Stadiums, in this topic

Bats, baseball player's right to recover for baseball-related personal injuries from nonplayer, **55 ALR4th 664, § 21**

Bludgeon, blackjack, or billy within meaning of criminal possession statute, what constitutes, **11 ALR4th 1272**

Bookmaking, validity, construction, and application of statutes or ordinances involved in prosecutions for possession of bookmaking paraphernalia, **51 ALR4th 796, § 7(a)**

Camps, liability of youth camp, its agents or employees, or of scouting leader or organization, for injury to child participant in program, **88 ALR3d 1236, § 9(b, c), 13(g), 18**

Consult POCKET PART for Later Annotations

BASEBALL—Cont'd

Schools and education

athletic events, tort liability of public schools and institutions of higher learning for accidents occurring during school athletic events, **68 ALR5th 663, § 3(a), 4(b), 5, 8, 9(b)**

physical education classes, tort liability of public schools and institutions of higher learning for accidents occurring in physical education classes, **66 ALR5th 1, § 3, 29, 32**

Spectators

assault, liability of owner or operator of theater or other amusement to patron assaulted by another patron, **75 ALR3d 441, § 16**

ball, liability to spectator at baseball game who is hit by ball or injured as result of other hazard of game, **91 ALR3d 24**

player's right to recover for baseball-related personal injuries from nonplayer, **55 ALR4th 664**

Stadiums

financing, validity of governmental borrowing or expenditure for purposes of acquiring, maintaining, or improving stadium for use of professional athletic team, **67 ALR3d 1186, § 7, 9**

lights, casting of light on another's premises as constituting actionable wrong, **5 ALR2d 1458**

spectators, in this topic

Sunday, construction of statute or ordinance prohibiting or regulating sports and games on, **24 ALR2d 813**

Third persons, baseball player's right to recover for baseball-related personal injuries from nonplayer, **55 ALR4th 664**

Trademarks, design on recreational object as valid trademark, **82 ALR Fed 9, § 3(b), 4(c, d), 9(a), 13(d)**

Umpire, referee, or judge of game or contest, liability for injury to or death of, **10 ALR3d 446**

Workers' compensation, award of workers' compensation benefits to profes-

BASEBALL—Cont'd

sional athletes, **112 ALR5th 365, § 7, 10, 11, 14, 18**

BASEMENTS AND FOUNDATIONS

Accessibility, way of necessity over another's land where a means of access does exist, but is claimed to be inadequate, inconvenient, difficult, or costly, **10 ALR4th 447, § 8(b), 14(b)**

Adverse possession based on encroachment of building or other structure, **2 ALR3d 1005, § 4, 8, 10**

Architect's liability for personal injury or death allegedly caused by improper or defective plans or design, **97 ALR3d 455, § 8(b)**

Brokers, real-estate broker's liability to purchaser for misrepresentation or nondisclosure of physical defects in property sold, **46 ALR4th 546, § 3, 6, 7, 14(c), 19(c)**

Collapse, what constitutes collapse of a building within coverage of property insurance policy, **71 ALR3d 1072, § 4**

Commencement of building or improvement for purposes of determining accrual of mechanic's lien, **1 ALR3d 822, § 3, 5 to 7, 10**

Damages, modern status of rule as to whether cost of correction or difference in value of structures is proper measure of damages for breach of construction contract, **41 ALR4th 131, § 56**

Drugs, conviction of possession of illicit drugs found in premises of which defendant was in nonexclusive possession, **56 ALR3d 948, § 10(b), 11**

Eviction, constructive eviction based on flooding, dampness, or the like, **33 ALR3d 1356, § 4, 6(b)**

Flooding

discovery rule, modern status of the application of "discovery rule" to postpone running of limitations against actions relating to breach of building and construction contracts, **33 ALR5th 1, § 4(a)**

eviction, constructive eviction based on flooding, dampness, or the like, **33 ALR3d 1356, § 4, 6(b)**

Consult POCKET PART for Later Annotations

ALR
INDEX

UPDATE
COVERING

ALR 6th, Vols. 36-92
ALR Fed 2d, Vols. 31-82
ALR Int'l, Vols. 1-7
ALR Electronic Annotations

ALSO CONTAINING
Annotation History Table

INDEX

A-B

Latest Case Service
For cases subsequent to publication of ALR supplements, call
1-800-225-7488

Issued April, 2014

THOMSON REUTERS™

Mat # 41385900

BARTON DOCTRINE

Bankruptcy, applicability of "Barton doctrine," providing that leave from appointing court required before filing suit against bankruptcy trustee, and effect or cure of violations thereof, **63 ALR Fed 2d 443**

BASEBALL

Antitrust laws, application of federal antitrust laws to professional sports, **79 ALR Fed 2d 1**

Comparative negligence

baseball player's right to recover for baseball-related personal injuries from nonplayer, **55 ALR4th 664, § 3(a)**

spectator, liability to spectator at baseball game who is hit by ball or injured as result of other hazards of game — failure to provide or maintain sufficient screening, **82 ALR6th 417**

Contact sports exception, construction and application of contact sports exception to negligence, **75 ALR6th 109, § 3, 4**

BASKETBALL

Antitrust laws, application of federal antitrust laws to professional sports, **79 ALR Fed 2d 1**

Contact sports exception, construction and application of contact sports exception to negligence.

BEACHES AN

Indecent exposu municipal ind and ordinances, **71 ALR6th 283, § 5, 10, 28, 29**

BEARS

Cruelty, challenges to pre- and post-conviction forfeitures and to postconviction restitution under animal cruelty statutes, **70 ALR6th 329, § 14**

Delisting of species protected under Endangered Species Act, **54 ALR Fed 2d 607, § 5, 8, 10, 12, 13**

Restitution, propriety, measure, and elements of restitution to which victim is entitled under state criminal statute —

BEARS—Cont'd

cruelty to, killing, or abandonment of, animals, **45 ALR6th 435, § 4, 12**

BEER

Interplay between Twenty-first Amendment and Sherman Act concerning state regulation of intoxicating liquors, **41 ALR6th 77**

BELARUS

Arbitration, construction and application of United Nations Convention on Recognition and Enforcement of Foreign Arbitral Awards, June 10, 1958, 330 U.N.T.S. 38, also known as the "New York Convention" — global cases: procedural matters, rules governing arbitration panel, evidentiary requirements, and motions related to Convention, **2 ALR Int'l 1, § 15, 16**

Asylum application, construction and application of 8 C.F.R. § 208.6 and 8 C.F.R. § 1208.6 prohibiting nonconsensual disclosure to third parties of information regarding asylum application, **39 ALR Fed 2d 189, § 5**

International sale of goods, construction and application of United Nations Convention on Contracts for the International Sale of Goods, April 10, 1980, 1489 U.N.T.S. 3

licability, 3

ach, remedation of ALR Int'l

505, § 19, 129

BELGIUM

Arbitration

investment disputes, construction, application, and interpretation of Washington Convention and ICSID Arbitration Rules and Additional Facility Rules through ICSID arbitral awards, **6 ALR Int'l 1, § 26**

United Nations Convention on Recognition and Enforcement of Foreign Arbitral Awards, June 10, 1958, 330 U.N.T.S. 38, also known as the

The newest articles are found in the pocket part supplement, including the on-point article for the legal issue being researched.

AMERICAN LAW REPORTS

ALR6th

Annotations and Cases

VOLUME 82

2013

 THOMSON REUTERS™

Mat #41245862

Liability to Spectator at Baseball Game Who Is Hit by Ball or Injured as Result of Other Hazards of Game—Failure to Provide or Maintain Sufficient Screening

by
Jay M. Zitter, J.D.

Part of the experience of attending a baseball game is that many of the dozens of baseballs used in each game are hit out of play into foul territory, into the backstop and screens, and into the stands. Most fans would love to return from a game with a souvenir of the actual play, and some even bring gloves with them in the hope of making a catch. Nevertheless, where attendees are hit by a baseball and injured, they frequently charge that the defendants should have provided more or better screens. Thus, in Edward C. v. City of Albuquerque, 2010-NMSC-043, 148 N.M. 646, 241 P.3d 1086, 82 A.L.R.6th 695 (2010), the Supreme Court of New Mexico ruled that spectators must exercise ordinary care to protect themselves from the inherent risk of being hit by a projectile that leaves the field of play, and the owner/occupant must exercise ordinary care not to increase that inherent risk, in holding that where a child was struck in the head by a baseball during pregame batting practice at a minor league stadium while the child was seated in the picnic area beyond the unscreened left field wall in fair ball territory with his family for a pregame Little League party, the defendants had not adduced sufficient evidence that there was not a genuine issue of material fact and that they were entitled to a judgment as a matter of law. Other courts have reached a variety of conclusions as to whether the stadium was liable to fans hurt by bats, balls, or the like, due to insufficient or inadequate screening, as the following annotation illustrates.

Edward C. v. City of Albuquerque is fully reported at page 695, infra.

TABLE OF CONTENTS

Research References

Index

Table of Cases, Laws, and Rules

Section 9 collects the cases on liability to a spectator at a baseball game who is hit by a ball due to the failure to provide or maintain sufficient screening at the picnic area of the baseball stadium.

Research References

The following references may be of related or collateral interest to a user of this annotation.

WEST'S KEY NUMBER DIGEST
Judgment ☞181(33); Negligence ☞333; Public Amusement and Entertainment ☞109(2), 128, 161; Schools ☞89.7

WESTLAW DATABASES
Art, Entertainment and Sports Law—Texts and Periodicals (AES-TP)
Art, Entertainment, and Sports Law—Texts & Periodicals Pro Plan Multibase (AES-TP-PRO)
Coach & Athletic Director (COACHATDIR)
Comparative Negligence Manual (COMPNEGMAN)
DePaul Journal of Sports Law & Contemporary Problems (DPLJSLCP)
Expert Witness Resumes (EXPTRESUME)
Handbook of Personal Injury Forms and Litigation Materials (HPIF)
Journal of Athletic Training (JATHTRAIN)
Journal of Legal Aspects of Sport (JLEGASP)
Litigating Tort Cases (LITGTORT)

question of whether the club was negligent in permitting practice very close to the grandstand was a question of fact for the jury.

§ 8 In dugout, players' bench area, or the like

Where a baseball spectator seated in the dugout, players' bench area, or the like was struck by a batted ball during the pregame practice, there is case law considering whether the evidence established or supported a finding that the owner or operator of the ballpark, the teams, or the like was liable for failing to provide sufficient screening.

Stating that as a matter of law a spectator assumes the risks necessarily incident to the baseball game so long as those risks are not unduly enhanced by the owner of the ballpark, the court, in Kozera v. Town of Hamburg, 40 A.D.2d 934, 337 **N.Y.S.2d** 761 (4th Dep't 1972), concluded that the father of a Little League ballplayer who was struck in the right eye by a foul ball during batting practice preceding a game assumed the risks incidental to batting practice at that ball game where he seated himself on the players' bench and was alerted to the danger by being compelled to duck a foul ball a few minutes before he was hit. In his complaint, the spectator alleged that the municipality was negligent in constructing, operating, and maintaining the baseball diamond and that there were inadequate facilities and equipment to provide protection for spectators at the playground and that there was improper supervision of the playing of baseball at the playground. Reversing a denial of summary judgment in favor of a municipality that owned and operated the baseball diamond, the court concluded that there was no triable fact issue with respect to maintenance and supervision of the playground area. The court pointed out that there was no evidence in the record as to any structural defect in the facility maintained by the municipality, nor was there any factual allegation with respect to a lack of supervision to be found in the record. The court pointed out that there was a screened area behind home plate where the spectator in this case could have watched the game and protected himself during batting practice had he so desired.

§ 9 In inner concourse, exit area, concession and picnic area, and the like

Where a baseball spectator seated in the inner concourse, exit area, concession and picnic area, and the like was struck by a batted ball during the pregame practice, under the particular circumstances of the following cases, the courts considered whether the evidence established or supported a finding that the owner or operator of the ballpark, the teams, or the like was liable for failing to provide sufficient screening.

Explaining that while spectators must exercise ordinary care to protect

444

themselves from the inherent risk of being hit by a projectile that leaves the field of play, the owner/occupant must exercise ordinary care not to increase that inherent risk, and was not exempt merely by supplying a screened area, in Edward C. v. City of Albuquerque, 2010-**NMSC**-043, 148 N.M. 646, 241 P.3d 1086, 82 A.L.R.6th 695 (2010), where a child was struck in the head by a baseball during pregame batting practice at a minor league stadium while the child was seated in the picnic area beyond the unscreened left field wall in fair ball territory with his family for a pregame Little League party, the court ruled that the defendants had not adduced sufficient evidence that there was not a genuine issue of material fact and that they were entitled to a judgment as a matter of law.

In Jones v. Three Rivers Management Corp., 483 **Pa.** 75, 394 A.2d 546 (1978), the court held that a verdict for a spectator who was struck by a foul ball during pregame batting practice, which ball came through an opening in a concourse used by ballpark patrons to move about the stadium, would not be disturbed since openings built into the walkway wall were not an inherent feature of spectator sport of baseball. The concourse circled the ballpark, and on the side of it facing the field, there was a wall about four feet high with about seven feet of open space above that, extending to the ceiling, which was apparently formed by a higher tier of seats; in the concourse were refreshment stands and restrooms. The spectator had been standing with a friend looking at the field but had decided to get something to eat; she had turned her back to the field and walked a few steps away from the wall when she was struck by the foul ball. The court explained that the rule that evidence that an injured party was exposed in the stands of a baseball stadium to the predictable risks of batted balls is not sufficient to establish, prima facie, a breach of the standard of care owed a baseball patron by a stadium operator was inapplicable in the present situation since one who attends a baseball game as a spectator cannot properly be charged with anticipating as inherent to baseball the risk of being struck by a baseball while properly using an interior walkway. The court reasoned that the openings built into the wall over right field were architectural features of the specific stadium which are not an inherent feature of the spectator sport of baseball as they were not compelled by or associated with the ordinary manner in which baseball is played or viewed and could not be characterized as part of the spectator sport of baseball. The court added that to determine whether the jury's verdict could stand, it was necessary to ascertain whether the spectator had established that the stadium had breached the standard of care owed the spectator and that the breach was the proximate cause of her injury. The court pointed out that the spectator was injured in an interior walkway and that its structure required patrons to turn their attention away from any activity on the field in order to safely navigate the concourse and that the spectator further testified that when she stopped to

445

look out into the field of play, she saw some activity on the field but was not aware that batting practice had begun and did not see home plate. The court said that it was for the jury to determine the question of negligence and that taking the evidence in the light most favorable to the spectator, it could not disturb the jury's verdict.

2. During Play of Game

§ 10 In stands, seating area, or the like—Liability held established or supportable

In the particular circumstances of the following cases, involving the liability of the owner or operator of a ballpark for failing to provide sufficient screening, the courts held that liability to a spectator struck by a batted ball during the course of the game was established or supportable.

Reversing a summary judgment in favor of a major league baseball club where a spectator was struck by a foul ball during a game while seated in an unscreened section of a stadium in the area near first base, in Rudnick v. Golden West Broadcasters, 156 **Cal. App.** 3d 793, 202 Cal. Rptr. 900 (4th Dist. 1984), the court held that an issue of material fact existed as to whether the stadium provided screened seats for as many spectators as might be reasonably expected to call for them on any ordinary occasion, precluding summary judgment. The stadium manager testified as to the size of the backstop screen, the composition of the screen, and that the screen covered approximately 2,300 seats. The court reasoned that the declaration of the stadium manager was insufficient to support the judgment as it utterly failed to demonstrate that screened seats were provided for as many fans as might be reasonably expected to call for them on any ordinary occasion. The court noted that the declaration's statement as to 2,300 screened seats did not mention a matter of common knowledge that the team regularly drew crowds 10 to 20 times that size. Moreover, the court continued, the declaration made no effort to correlate the number of screened seats with the number of requests reasonably to be expected for them and did not allege any screened seats were truly available to fans who were not longtime season ticket holders.

In Jackson v. Atlanta Braves, Inc., 227 So. 2d 63 (**Fla. 4th DCA** 1969), the court reversed a summary judgment in favor of a baseball club and a city in an action by a spectator who was struck by a foul ball that was tipped over the vertical backstop behind home plate. The complaint charged the city, the owner of the stadium, and the baseball club, to which the stadium was leased, with failing to provide an adequate screening behind home plate. The court concluded that while there did not appear to be a substantial conflict in the evidentiary facts, various conclusions might reasonably be drawn as to the ultimate factual issues of negligence, contributory negligence, and assumption of risk.

446

4.   United States Code Annotated

U.S.C.A. Problem

Government agents observed a man in his parked car talking on his cell phone. Later, the agents observed other cars drive up to the man's car and stop. The man handed each driver a brown paper bag in exchange for money. After observing this activity, the agents questioned the man and searched his car. They found cocaine, a controlled substance, in the man's car.

Is there any authority in the U.S. Code for forfeiture of the man's car?

Worksheet

Parties:

Places and Things:

Basis of Action or Issue:

Defense:

Relief Sought:

UNITED STATES CODE ANNOTATED

2013
GENERAL INDEX
J to R

The United States Code Annotated General Index is an alphabetical subject matter index that includes all subjects covered in the entire U.S.C.A. set. There is also an index located at the end of many titles of the U.S.C.A., containing only subjects covered in that title. These indexes are a great place to start your research when you are unsure where your issue is addressed in the statutes.

THOMSON REUTERS

Mat #41269362

Under Motor Vehicles, the general index contains an entry on forfeitures related to controlled substances, directing you to 21 U.S.C.A. § 881.

UNITED STATES CODE ANNOTATED

TITLE 21

Food and Drugs

§§ 848 to 950

Comprising All Laws of a General
and Permanent Nature
Under Arrangement of the Official Code of
the Laws of the United States
with
Annotations from Federal Courts

The United States Code Annotated includes the text of the statutes, as well as relevant annotations such as law review and journal commentaries, various references to legal encyclopedias and treatises, and other research materials. References also include notes of decisions from relevant case law, organized by topic. Included in this book is 21 U.S.C.A. § 881, which deals with forfeitures in drug cases.

585 F.2d 69. Criminal Law ⚖ 392.15(8)

Where subsequent statements made by defendant were directly related to information gathered by Drug Enforcement

Agency compliance officers as result of illegal search of defendant's pharmacy, defendant was entitled to suppression of such statements. U. S. v. Enserro, W.D.N.Y.1975, 401 F.Supp. 460. Criminal Law ⚖ 413.13

§ 881. Forfeitures

(a) Subject property

The following shall be subject to forfeiture to the United States and no property right shall exist in them:

(1) All controlled substances which have been manufactured, distributed, dispensed, or acquired in violation of this subchapter.

(2) All raw materials, products, and equipment of any kind which are used, or intended for use, in manufacturing, compounding, processing, delivering, importing, or exporting any controlled substance or listed chemical in violation of this subchapter.

(3) All property which is used, or intended for use, as a container for property described in paragraph (1), (2), or (9).

(4) All conveyances, including aircraft, vehicles, or vessels, which are used, or are intended for use, to transport, or in any manner to facilitate the transportation, sale, receipt, possession, or concealment of property described in paragraph (1), (2), or (9).

(5) All books, records, and research, including formulas, microfilm, tapes, and data which are used, or intended for use, in violation of this subchapter.

(6) All moneys, negotiable instruments, securities, or other things of value furnished by any person in exchange for a controlled substance or listed chemical in violation of this subchapter, all proceeds traceable to such an exchange, and all moneys, negotiable instruments, and securities used or intended to be used to facilitate any violation of this subchapter.

> Here, the statute provides that vehicles used to facilitate the sale of controlled substances are subject to forfeiture.

(7) All real property, including any right, title, and interest (including any leasehold interest) in the whole of any lot or tract of land and any appurtenances or improvements, which is used, or intended to be used, in any manner or part, to commit, or to facilitate the commission of, a violation of this subchapter punishable by more than one year's imprisonment.

(8) All controlled substances which have been possessed in violation of this subchapter.

356

(9) All listed chemicals, all drug manufacturing equipment, all tableting machines, all encapsulating machines, and all gelatin capsules, which have been imported, exported, manufactured, possessed, distributed, dispensed, acquired, or intended to be distributed, dispensed, acquired, imported, or exported, in violation of this subchapter or subchapter II of this chapter.

(10) Any drug paraphernalia (as defined in section 863 of this title).

(11) Any firearm (as defined in section 921 of Title 18) used or intended to be used to facilitate the transportation, sale, receipt, possession, or concealment of property described in paragraph (1) or (2) and any proceeds traceable to such property.

(b) Seizure procedures

Any property subject to forfeiture to the United States under this section may be seized by the Attorney General in the manner set forth in section 981(b) of Title 18.

(c) Custody of Attorney General

Property taken or detained under this section shall not be repleviable, but shall be deemed to be in the custody of the Attorney General, subject only to the orders and decrees of the court or the official having jurisdiction thereof. Whenever property is seized under any of the provisions of this subchapter, the Attorney General may—

(1) place the property under seal;

(2) remove the property to a place designated by him; or

(3) require that the General Services Administration take custody of the property and remove it, if practicable, to an appropriate location for disposition in accordance with law.

(d) Other laws and proceedings applicable

The provisions of law relating to the seizure, summary and judicial forfeiture, and condemnation of property for violation of the customs laws; the disposition of such property or the proceeds from the sale thereof; the remission or mitigation of such forfeitures; and the compromise of claims shall apply to seizures and forfeitures incurred, or alleged to have been incurred, under any of the provisions of this subchapter, insofar as applicable and not inconsistent with the provisions hereof; except that such duties as are imposed upon the customs officer or any other person with respect to the seizure and forfeiture of property under the customs laws shall be performed with respect to seizures and forfeitures of property under this subchapter by such officers, agents, or other persons as may be authorized or designated for that purpose by the Attorney General, except to

357

the extent that such duties arise from seizures and forfeitures effected by any customs officer.

(e) Disposition of forfeited property

(1) Whenever property is civilly or criminally forfeited under this subchapter the Attorney General may—

(A) retain the property for official use or, in the manner provided with respect to transfers under section 1616a of Title 19, transfer the property to any Federal agency or to any State or local law enforcement agency which participated directly in the seizure or forfeiture of the property;

(B) except as provided in paragraph (4), sell, by public sale or any other commercially feasible means, any forfeited property which is not required to be destroyed by law and which is not harmful to the public;

(C) require that the General Services Administration take custody of the property and dispose of it in accordance with law;

(D) forward it to the Bureau of Narcotics and Dangerous Drugs for disposition (including delivery for medical or scientific use to any Federal or State agency under regulations of the Attorney General); or

(E) transfer the forfeited personal property or the proceeds of the sale of any forfeited personal or real property to any foreign country which participated directly or indirectly in the seizure or forfeiture of the property, if such a transfer—

(i) has been agreed to by the Secretary of State;

(ii) is authorized in an international agreement between the United States and the foreign country; and

(iii) is made to a country which, if applicable, has been certified under section 2291j(b) of Title 22.

(2)(A) The proceeds from any sale under subparagraph (B) of paragraph (1) and any moneys forfeited under this subchapter shall be used to pay—

(i) all property expenses of the proceedings for forfeiture and sale including expenses of seizure, maintenance of custody, advertising, and court costs; and

(ii) awards of up to $100,000 to any individual who provides original information which leads to the arrest and conviction of a person who kills or kidnaps a Federal drug law enforcement agent.

Any award paid for information concerning the killing or kidnapping of a Federal drug law enforcement agent, as provided in clause (ii), shall be paid at the discretion of the Attorney General.

358

(B) The Attorney General shall forward to the Treasurer of the United States for deposit in accordance with section 524(c) of Title 28, any amounts of such moneys and proceeds remaining after payment of the expenses provided in subparagraph (A), except that, with respect to forfeitures conducted by the Postal Service, the Postal Service shall deposit in the Postal Service Fund, under section 2003(b)(7) of Title 39, such moneys and proceeds.

(3) The Attorney General shall assure that any property transferred to a State or local law enforcement agency under paragraph (1)(A)—

(A) has a value that bears a reasonable relationship to the degree of direct participation of the State or local agency in the law enforcement effort resulting in the forfeiture, taking into account the total value of all property forfeited and the total law enforcement effort with respect to the violation of law on which the forfeiture is based; and

(B) will serve to encourage further cooperation between the recipient State or local agency and Federal law enforcement agencies.

(4)(A) With respect to real property described in subparagraph (B), if the chief executive officer of the State involved submits to the Attorney General a request for purposes of such subparagraph, the authority established in such subparagraph is in lieu of the authority established in paragraph (1)(B).

(B) In the case of property described in paragraph (1)(B) that is civilly or criminally forfeited under this subchapter, if the property is real property that is appropriate for use as a public area reserved for recreational or historic purposes or for the preservation of natural conditions, the Attorney General, upon the request of the chief executive officer of the State in which the property is located, may transfer title to the property to the State, either without charge or for a nominal charge, through a legal instrument providing that—

(i) such use will be the principal use of the property; and

(ii) title to the property reverts to the United States in the event that the property is used otherwise.

(f) Forfeiture and destruction of schedule I and II substances

(1) All controlled substances in schedule I or II that are possessed, transferred, sold, or offered for sale in violation of the provisions of this subchapter; all dangerous, toxic, or hazardous raw materials or products subject to forfeiture under subsection (a)(2) of this section; and any equipment or container subject to forfeiture under subsection (a)(2) or (3) of this section which cannot be separated safely from such raw materials or products shall be deemed contraband and seized and summarily forfeited to the United States. Similarly,

359

all substances in schedule I or II, which are seized or come into the possession of the United States, the owners of which are unknown, shall be deemed contraband and summarily forfeited to the United States.

(2) The Attorney General may direct the destruction of all controlled substances in schedule I or II seized for violation of this subchapter; all dangerous, toxic, or hazardous raw materials or products subject to forfeiture under subsection (a)(2) of this section; and any equipment or container subject to forfeiture under subsection (a)(2) or (3) of this section which cannot be separated safely from such raw materials or products under such circumstances as the Attorney General may deem necessary.

(g) Plants

(1) All species of plants from which controlled substances in schedules I and II may be derived which have been planted or cultivated in violation of this subchapter, or of which the owners or cultivators are unknown, or which are wild growths, may be seized and summarily forfeited to the United States.

(2) The failure, upon demand by the Attorney General or his duly authorized agent, of the person in occupancy or in control of land or premises upon which such species of plants are growing or being stored, to produce an appropriate registration, or proof that he is the holder thereof, shall constitute authority for the seizure and forfeiture.

(3) The Attorney General, or his duly authorized agent, shall have authority to enter upon any lands, or into any dwelling pursuant to a search warrant, to cut, harvest, carry off, or destroy such plants.

(h) Vesting of title in United States

All right, title, and interest in property described in subsection (a) of this section shall vest in the United States upon commission of the act giving rise to forfeiture under this section.

(i) Stay of civil forfeiture proceedings

The provisions of section 981(g) of Title 18 regarding the stay of a civil forfeiture proceeding shall apply to forfeitures under this section.

(j) Venue

In addition to the venue provided for in section 1395 of Title 28 or any other provision of law, in the case of property of a defendant charged with a violation that is the basis for forfeiture of the property under this section, a proceeding for forfeiture under this section may

360

be brought in the judicial district in which the defendant owning such property is found or in the judicial district in which the criminal prosecution is brought.

(*l*) [1] **Agreement between Attorney General and Postal Service for performance of functions**

The functions of the Attorney General under this section shall be carried out by the Postal Service pursuant to such agreement as may be entered into between the Attorney General and the Postal Service.

(Pub.L. 91–513, Title II, § 511, Oct. 27, 1970, 84 Stat. 1276; Pub.L. 95–633, Title III, § 301(a), Nov. 10, 1978, 92 Stat. 3777; Pub.L. 96–132, § 14, Nov. 30, 1979, 93 Stat. 1048; Pub.L. 98–473, Title II, §§ 306, 309, 518, Oct. 12, 1984, 98 Stat. 2050, 2051, 2075; Pub.L. 99–570, Title I, §§ 1006(c), 1865, 1992, Oct. 27, 1986, 100 Stat. 3207-7, 3207-54, 3207-59; Pub.L. 99–646, § 74, Nov. 10, 1986, 100 Stat. 3618; Pub.L. 100–690, Title V, § 5105, Title VI, §§ 6059, 6074, 6075, 6077(a), (b), 6253, Nov. 18, 1988, 102 Stat. 4301, 4319, 4323–4325, 4363; Pub.L. 101–189, Div. A, Title XII, § 1215(a), Nov. 29, 1989, 103 Stat. 1569; Pub.L. 101–647, Title XX, §§ 2003, 2004, 2007, 2008, Nov. 29, 1990, 104 Stat. 4855, 4856; Pub.L. 102–239, § 2, Dec. 17, 1991, 105 Stat. 1912; Pub.L. 102–583, § 6(a), Nov. 2, 1992, 106 Stat. 4932; Pub.L. 103–447, Title I, §§ 102(d), 103(a), Nov. 2, 1994, 108 Stat. 4693; Pub.L. 104–237, Title II, § 201(b), Oct. 3, 1996, 110 Stat. 3101; Pub.L. 106–185, §§ 2(c)(2), 5(b), 8(b), Apr. 25, 2000, 114 Stat. 210, 214, 216; Pub.L. 107–273, Div. B, Title IV, § 4002(e)(3), Nov. 2, 2002, 116 Stat. 1810.)

[1] So in original.   No subsec. (k) has been enacted.

HISTORICAL AND STATUTORY NOTES

Revision Notes and Legislative Reports

1970 Acts. House Report No. 91–1444 and Conference Report No. 91–1603, see 1970 U.S. Code Cong. and Adm. News, p. 4566.

1978 Acts. House Report No. 95–1193, see 1978 U.S. Code Cong. and Adm. News, p. 9496.

1979 Acts. Senate Report No. 96–173 and House Conference Report No. 96–628, see 1979 U.S. Code Cong. and Adm. News, p. 2003.

1984 Acts. House Report No. 98–1030 and House Conference Report No. 98–1159, see 1984 U.S. Code Cong. and Adm. News, p. 3182.

1986 Acts. Statement by President, see 1986 U.S. Code Cong. and Adm. News, p. 5393.

House Report No. 99–797, see 1986 U.S. Code Cong. and Adm. News, p. 6138.

1988 Acts. For Related Reports, see 1988 U.S. Code Cong. and Adm. News, p. 5937.

1989 Acts. House Report No. 101–121, House Conference Report No. 101–331, and Statement by President, see 1989 U.S. Code Cong. and Adm. News, p. 838.

1990 Acts. House Report Nos. 101–681(Parts I and II), 101–736, Senate Report No. 101–460, and Statement by President, see 1990 U.S. Code Cong. and Adm. News, p. 6472.

1991 Acts. House Report No. 102–359, and Statement by President, see 1991 U.S. Code Cong. and Adm. News, p. 1518.

1994 Acts. Related House Report No. 103–724, see 1994 U.S. Code Cong. and Adm. News, p. 3682.

2002 Acts. House Conference Report No. 107–685 and Statement by President, see 2002 U.S. Code Cong. and Adm. News, p. 1120.

References in Text

"This subchapter", referred to in text, was in the original "this title" which is Title II of Pub.L. 91–513, Oct. 27, 1970, 84 Stat. 1242, and is popularly known as

361

Notes of Decisions

Under the Notes of Decisions feature, there is a list of topical headings to help you find relevant cases. Here, there is a topical heading for motor vehicles.

376

ried on in vehicle, automobile was not subject to forfeiture under this section providing for forfeiture of vehicles used to facilitate sale of contraband.   U.S. v. One 1972 Datsun, Vehicle Identification No. LB1100355950, D.C.N.H.1974, 378 F.Supp. 1200.

Automobile which was used to transport money to pay for completed shipments of marijuana and to pay for renting airplane which was used to fly marijuana in from Mexico "facilitated" the importation, transportation and sale of marijuana even though no marijuana was found in the automobile.   U.S. v. One 1973 Volvo, W.D.Tex.1974, 377 F.Supp. 810.

Mere use of automobile as first link in chain of transportation of person to Mexico for purpose of buying heroin was not "facilitation" within this section providing that vehicles used to facilitate transportation, sale, receipt, possession or concealment of controlled substances are subje[...]ates.   U.S. [...]rial No. [...]973, 374 F[...]

21.   [...]

Mo[...]jua-
na wa[...]s of statute p[...]vey-
ances used to trans[...]ort controlled substances, as that stat[...]e was intended to connote "conveyance" that is really mobile in everyday ter[...]s, and not in sense of cumbersome and rare movement of mobile home.   U.S. v One 1989 Stratford Fairmont 14' x 7[...] Mob[...]e Home, Located at 290 Susan [...], Park City, Ill., N.D.Ill.1992, 783 F.[...]pp. 1154, affirmed 986 F.2d 177, rehear[...]g denied.

Cases addressing forfeitures of motor vehicles are found here.

22.   —— Motor vehicles, conveyances
Motor vehicle used by suspect to drive to and from meeting at which suspect instructed undercover agent to obtain passport and agreed to pay agent $10,000 for transporting heroin into country was subject to forfeiture as conveyance for use to facilitate transportation of heroin.   U.S. v. 1990 Toyota 4Runner, C.A.7 (Ill.) 1993, 9 F.3d 651.   Controlled Substances ⟱ 171

Use of vehicle only for transportation of owner to site of illegal narcotics transaction was sufficient to warrant forfeiture of vehicle, even under "substantial connection" standard; use of vehicle to transport its owner to pawn shop facili-

tated transaction by enabling owner to consummate purchase which she prearranged by telephone call.   U.S. v. One 1984 Cadillac, C.A.6 (Ky.) 1989, 888 F.2d 1133.

Although automobile was properly forfeited to government on basis of its use in violation of drug control laws, automobile telephone attached to automobile, which was easily removable, had identity and use separate from automobile, and was separately insured, was not subject to forfeiture with automobile itself, especially where there was no evidence that telephone was used in furtherance of underlying crime.   U.S. v. One 1978 Mercedes Benz, Four-Door Sedan, VIN: 116-036-12-004084, C.A.5 (Tex.) 1983, 711 F.2d 1297.

Although subject's automobile had transported neither contraband nor money, the vehicle, which was used to transport the pivotal figure in the attempted narcotics transaction several hundred miles to the precise location in which the attempted purchase took place, had a sufficient nexus to the attempted drug purchase to support the forfeiture.   U.S. v. One 1979 Porsche Coupe, VIN 9289200514, C.A.11 (Ga.) 1983, 709 F.2d 1424.

A vehicle may be seized if there is probable cause to believe that it was used or was intended for use to facilitate transportation of contraband.   U.S. v. Ogden, C.A.1 (Me.) 1983, 703 F.2d 629.

Where automobile of defendant charged with possession with intent to distribute and distribution of marijuana had been used in connection with distribution of drugs, automobile, under this section, was already property of United States and it only remained for government to assert its right to immediate possession.   U.S. v. Kemp, C.A.4 (Md.) 1982, 690 F.2d 397.

Evidence that owner of automobile and codefendant drove automobile from McAllen to Midland to find an airstrip upon which airplane bringing in marijuana could land, that they drove it to find a storage building for the marijuana and to rent a motor home in which to live while selling the marijuana, that two of the conspirators drove the automobile to Midland to rent a truck, and that one of the conspirators planned to take marijuana samples to Dallas in the automobile established a sufficient nexus between the

UNITED STATES CODE ANNOTATED

Title 21
Food and Drugs
§§ 848 to End

2013
Cumulative Annual Pocket Part

Replacing 2012 pocket part in the back of 1999 bound volume

Includes the Laws of the
112th CONGRESS, Second Session (2012)

For close of Notes of Decisions
See page III

For Later Laws and Cases
Consult
USCA
Interim Pamphlet Service

The Cumulative Annual Pocket Part contains updates to the statutory text and annotations located in a specific volume of the U.S.C.A. The pocket part is a loose pamphlet inserted in the back of the volume. To ensure that your research includes the most current statutory text available and the most recent annotations, you must look at the text and annotations in both the bound volume and the pocket part. In addition, you should check for any interim pamphlets. An interim pamphlet is a separate soft cover pamphlet located at the end of the statutory set. Only updates to the bound volume will appear in the pocket part or interim pamphlet, so if the section you are researching does not appear in the pocket part or interim pamphlet, the most current information is contained in the bound volume.

Federal Procedure, Lawyers Edition § 22:1652, Return of Findings.

Federal Procedure, Lawyers Edition § 37:1269, Seizure and Forfeiture.

Federal Procedure, Lawyers Edition § 37:1270, Seizure and Forfeiture--In Connection With Suspension or Revocation of Penalty.

Restatement (Third) of Agency § 5.03, Imputation of Notice of Fact to Principal.

Restatement (Third) of Agency § 5.03, Imputation of Notice of Fact to Principal.

Restatement (Third) of Agency § 5.03, Imputation of Notice of Fact to Principal.

Restatement (Third) of Agency § 5.03, Imputation of Notice of Fact to Principal.

Wright & Miller: Federal Prac. & Proc. § 126, Nature and Contents of the Indictment or Information--Criminal Forfeitures.

Wright & Miller: Federal Prac. & Proc. § 1074, The Requirement of Reasonable Notice.

Wright & Miller: Federal Prac. & Proc. § 3578, Fines, Penalties, Seizures, and Forfeitures.

Wright & Miller: Federal Prac. & Proc. § 3654, Jurisdiction Over Actions Against the United States.

Wright & Miller: Federal Prac. & Proc. § 3657, Statutory Exceptions to Sovereign Immunity--Actions Under the Tucker Act.

Wright & Miller: Federal Prac. & Proc. § 3820, Particular Classes of Cases--Fines, Penalties, Seizures, and Forfeitures.

Notes of Decisions

Constitutionality 1-4a
   Self-incrimination 4a
Rooker-Feldman doctrine 183
Self-incrimination, constitutionality 4a

---

1. Constitutionality—Generally

Evidence about claimant's medical condition and medicinal use of marijuana, including his asserted suicide attempt, was not relevant to issue of whether civil forfeiture pursuant to Controlled Substances Act (CSA) of property claimant used to cultivate marijuana violated Excessive Fines Clause, and thus was inadmissible in civil forfeiture action. U.S. v. One Parcel of Property Located at 5 Reynolds Lane, Waterford, Conn., D.Conn.2012, 2012 WL 6606597. Controlled Substances ⟐ 184; Fines ⟐ 1.3

Claimant opposing forfeiture of currency found in vehicle in which he was passenger could not refuse to answer deposition questions regarding funds, on Fifth Amendment grounds, and then assert that funds had nothing to do with drug transactions. U.S. v. U.S. Currency in Sum of One Hundred Eighty-Five Thousand Dollars ($185,000), E.D.N.Y.2006, 455 F.Supp.2d 145. Witnesses ⟐ 309

County, city, director of cooperative formed to provide marijuana to qualified patients, and cooperative's members failed to show likelihood of success on claim that enforcement of Controlled Substances Act (CSA) violated their Fifth and Ninth Amendment rights, as required for preliminary injunction in action against Drug Enforcement Administration (DEA) administrator and other officials after DEA agents seized marijuana plants from cooperative; rights claimed by plaintiffs, including to maintain bodily integrity, alleviate pain, and control circumstances of their deaths, were not rooted in history and tradition, and recognition of such rights was inconsistent with prior law. County of Santa Cruz, Cal. v. Ashcroft, N.D.Cal.2003, 279 F.Supp.2d 1192, on reconsideration 314 F.Supp.2d 1000. Injunction ⟐ 1401; Injunction ⟐ 1494

2. —— Due process, constitutionality

Procedure used by Federal Bureau of Investigation (FBI) to provide notice of administrative forfeiture of cash seized during search of residence where claimant had been arrested was reasonable under the circumstances, and thus satisfied due process requirements, where FBI sent letters of intention to forfeit cash by certified mail to claimant in care of federal correctional institution (FCI) where he was being held, to address of residence where he had been arrested, and to address in town where his mother lived, and also placed legal notice required by statute in newspaper published in district where forfeiture proceeding was brought; abrogating *Yeung Mung Weng v. United States*, 137 F.3d 709, and *United States v. Woodall*, 12 F.3d 791. Dusenbery v. U.S., U.S. 2002, 122 S.Ct. 694, 534 U.S. 161, 151 L.Ed.2d 597. Constitutional Law ⟐ 4078; Forfeitures ⟐ 5

Declaration of forfeiture of vehicle seized at time of defendant's arrest in drug conspiracy violated his due process rights where the notice of forfeiture was sent to correctional facility from which defendant was transferred less than two weeks before the notice was sent; the notice was not reasonably calculated under all the circumstances to apprise defendant of the forfeiture of the vehicle. Alli-Balogun v. U.S., C.A.2 (N.Y.) 2002, 281 F.3d 362.

Sovereign immunity precluded claimants whose real property was civilly forfeited in violation of due process from recovering value of property, as opposed to property itself or lost rents and profits, under civil forfeiture statute governing return of property wrongfully seized; replacement value would constitute prohibited consequential damages. U.S. v. 1461 West 42nd Street, Hialeah, Fla., C.A.11 (Fla.) 2001, 251 F.3d 1329, rehearing and rehearing en banc denied 31 Fed.Appx. 927, 2001 WL 1729151. United States ⟐ 125(9)

Due process requirements of predeprivation notice and meaningful opportunity to be heard did not apply to seizure of claimants' home appliances and furniture as personal property subject to civil forfeiture, inasmuch as such items were sufficiently mobile to justify ex parte seizure. U.S. v. All Assets and Equipment of West Side Bldg. Corp., C.A.7 (Ill.) 1999, 188 F.3d 440. Constitutional Law ⟐ 4078; Forfeitures ⟐ 5

Government did not have to alert fugitive of pending forfeiture when it later discovered him, and thereby spoil element of surprise in appre-

not constitute excessive fine against building's owner, who was defendant's mother; owner's conduct, i.e. her willful blindness to defendant's conduct, constituted violation of statute prohibiting maintaining of drug-involved premises, potential statutory fine would exceed value of forfeited property, and harm to public arising from willful blindness was substantial. U.S. v. Collado, C.A.2 (N.Y.) 2003, 348 F.3d 323, certiorari denied 124 S.Ct. 1620, 541 U.S. 904, 158 L.Ed.2d 246. Fines ⚖ 1.3

Court of Federal Claims's Tucker Act jurisdiction of mortgagee's claim that challenged propriety of in rem administrative forfeiture of mortgaged property seized was preempted by forfeiture provisions of the Controlled Substances Act, since statutory scheme established by the Controlled Substances Act provided complete administrative review by the Drug Enforcement Administration (DEA) and judicial review in district court. Vereda, Ltda. v. U.S., C.A.Fed.2001, 271 F.3d 1367.

No evidence showed that Congress intended for removal jurisdiction to be available to parties defending against common law claims, the success of which arguably required consideration of Federal Food, Drug, and Cosmetic Act (FDCA) or Controlled Substances Act (CSA), as would support removal of products liability action against drug manufacturers under substantial federal question and complete preemption doctrines; Acts did not replace entire state products liability cause of action, and the action sought money damages, rather than to overturn prior Food and Drug Administration (FDA) decisions regarding drug OxyContin. Little v. Purdue Pharma, L.P., S.D.Ohio 2002, 227 F.Supp.2d 838. Removal Of Cases ⚖ 19(1); Removal Of Cases ⚖ 25(1)

Claimant alleging that federal government wrongfully seized excess criminal forfeiture proceeds for his violation of CSA was not afforded right to money damages, under CSA's criminal forfeiture provisions, as required for money-mandating claim within Court of Federal Claims' Tucker Act jurisdiction, and thus, district court had exclusive jurisdiction over claim, pursuant to CSA's preemptive scheme for review of forfeiture actions, including challenges to both seizure itself and to excessive proceeds. Fischer v. U.S., Fed.Cl.2011, 96 Fed.Cl. 70, appeal dismissed 419 Fed.Appx. 991, 2011 WL 1530640. Federal Courts ⚖ 1139

Customs statute which authorizes rewards to informants who aid in the prosecution of customs law violations is not incorporated into drug forfeiture provisions. Emmens v. U.S., Fed.Cl. 1999, 44 Fed.Cl. 524. Customs Duties ⚖ 136

12. Ownership

State law must be referenced to determine the extent of forfeiture claimants' ownership interests under the Civil Asset Forfeiture Reform Act of 2000 (CAFRA); the non-exhaustive list of ownership interests included in CAFRA cannot supplant the role of state law in defining when and under what circumstances ownership interests in real property arise. U.S. v. 392 Lexington Parkway South, St. Paul, Minn.,

Ramsey County, D.Minn.2005, 386 F.Supp.2d 1062. Federal Courts ⚖ 433

13. Property subject to forfeiture

On claimants' motion for return of property, evidence was sufficient to support district court's findings that subject property constituted proceeds from the sale of drugs and, therefore, at all times, title to the property was vested in the government; agent who performed financial investigation on the drug organization and its businesses testified that the approximate revenue realized by the organization was $68 to $70 million, claimants' expenditures far exceeded their legal sources of income, and, although the claimants' won one million dollars in a horse race, the horse was purchased with drug proceeds. U.S. v. Rodriguez-Aguirre, C.A.10 (N.M.) 2005, 414 F.3d 1177. Controlled Substances ⚖ 156

Vehicle owner incarcerated after pleading no contest to state charges related to drug dealing was not entitled to relief from civil forfeiture of vehicle for its connection to transport of controlled substances on hardship grounds, where owner was incarcerated and would not endure any additional hardship from inability to drive vehicle. U.S. v. One 2001 Mercedes Benz ML 320, E.D.Wis.2009, 668 F.Supp.2d 1132, as amended. Controlled Substances ⚖ 165

18. —— Connection with offense, conveyances

Claimant's vehicle was substantially connected to claimant's criminal activity of possession of a

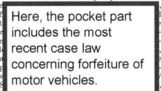

Here, the pocket part includes the most recent case law concerning forfeiture of motor vehicles.

Substances ⚖ 171

19. —— Facilitation, conveyances

Claimant's driving vehicles to planning meetings for drug transaction "facilitated" sale of drugs, even if vehicles themselves were not used to transport drugs, as required for vehicles to be subject to forfeiture. U.S. v. One Dodge Durango 2004, D.Puerto Rico 2006, 545 F.Supp.2d 197. Controlled Substances ⚖ 171

22. —— Motor vehicles, conveyances

Where owner was caught driving her vehicle with deliverable quantity of drugs and cash and was convicted of drug dealing, the vehicle was subject to civil forfeiture on ground it was used to transport controlled substances, even if owner drove vehicle in normal course of her daily life and drug dealing was not the primary purpose of the vehicle and even if vehicle was not being used for drug trafficking when owner was stopped. U.S. v. One 2001 Mercedes Benz ML 320, E.D.Wis.2009, 668 F.Supp.2d 1132, as amended. Controlled Substances ⚖ 171

112

Petitioner did not have right to lawful possession of administratively forfeited vehicle and equitable right to its return, where jury found in related criminal trial that petitioner purchased vehicle with narcotics proceeds in effort to conceal and disguise true source of such funds, and that petitioner conspired to purchase 7 1/2 kilograms of heroin in amount of $990,000. Concepcion v. U.S., E.D.N.Y.2004, 298 F.Supp.2d 351. Controlled Substances ⊂= 190

24. Money—Generally

Money that government seized in lawful search of defendant's home was subject to forfeiture, where money was found together with a large quantity of illegal drugs, a digital scale, and other evidence of drug trafficking. U.S. v. Cook, C.A.7 (Wis.) 2005, 406 F.3d 485. Controlled Substances ⊂= 171

Government showed by preponderance of the evidence that $60,020 in currency seized from airline passenger was substantially connected to narcotics trafficking, as required for forfeiture under Controlled Substances Act; evidence showed passenger disobeyed transportation security officer's direction to empty his pockets during airport security screening, and when TSO felt bulge in passenger's pocket during patdown search, passenger said it was a book, but it was revealed to be bricks of cash that were wrapped, taped, and bound in rubber bands, and drug-detection dog alerted to odor of methyl benzoate, a chemical by-product of cocaine, on the currency, and passenger provided conflicting, inconsistent, and vague answers as to how much money he was carrying and origin of the money. U.S. v. $60,020.00 U.S. Currency, W.D.N.Y.2011, 2011 WL 4720741. Controlled Substances ⊂= 171

Defendant property in forfeiture in rem proceeding, namely, $4,620 in United States currency, was used or intended to be used to facilitate violation of Controlled Substances Act (CSA), and thus property was forfeitable to government, where government provided sufficient notice of seizure of defendant property, only claim to property had been stricken for claimant's default, and time for filing claim to property had expired with no other claimants to property. U.S. v. $4,620 in U.S. Currency, D.D.C.2011, 779 F.Supp.2d 65. Controlled Substances ⊂= 171; Controlled Substances ⊂= 181

Government's failure to quiet title to cash seized during drug sting operation by means of civil forfeiture proceeding did not automatically vest title to the cash in the individual from whom it was seized, and government was entitled to retain the property until claimant filed equitable action or motion and demonstrated that he was lawfully entitled to the return of the property. Babb v. U.S. Drug Enforcement Agency, C.A.4 (S.C.) 2005, 146 Fed.Appx. 614, 2005 WL 2053349, Unreported, on subsequent appeal 231 Fed.Appx. 262, 2007 WL 1880031. Controlled Substances ⊂= 156

26. —— Proceeds, money

Preponderance of evidence supported finding that entire amount of $185,336.07 in United States currency seized from claimant was trace-able to contemporaneous drug trafficking activities to which claimant pleaded guilty in state court, and thus amount was forfeitable to government as drug proceeds in action seeking in rem forfeiture of funds; undisputed evidence demonstrated that claimant had engaged in drug trafficking, no evidence had pointed to legitimate source for seized funds, and claimant had failed to file tax returns showing legitimately-derived source of income. U.S. v. Sum of $185,336.07 U.S. Currency Seized from Citizen's Bank Account L7N-01967, W.D.N.Y.2012, 2012 WL 1523855. Controlled Substances ⊂= 165

The $13,000 in currency seized from a drug defendant's residence where the claimant, who was the defendant's mother, also resided was subject to civil forfeiture as proceeds of drug trafficking; the currency was packaged in a latex "rubbery bag" that was largely impermeable to gas and commonly used to conceal the smell of drugs and avoid detection by drug dogs. U.S. V. $13,000.00 in U.S. Currency, 2007 Black Dodge Ram SRT Pickup, VIN 1D7HA18257S120375, D.Colo.2012, 2012 WL 871203. Controlled Substances ⊂= 165

Currency in the amount of $21,055 was forfeitable to the government, on ground that it constituted moneys furnished or intended to be furnished in exchange for controlled substances, proceeds traceable to such an exchange, or used or intended to be used to facilitate a violation of the Controlled Substances Act; currency was found in sleeper area of claimant's commercial truck during truck inspection, in one plastic-wrapped bundle containing two individual rubber-banded bundles, which was type of wrapping commonly associated with transporting drug proceeds, drug dog alerted to odor of controlled substances on the currency, and claimant's reported adjusted gross income on two prior tax returns was $21,114 and $26,084. U.S. v. $21,055.00 in U.S. Currency, D.Kan.2011, 778 F.Supp.2d 1099. Controlled Substances ⊂= 165; Controlled Substances ⊂= 171

Government demonstrated by a preponderance of the evidence that money in Colombian bank accounts was subject to civil forfeiture since those funds could be traced to illegal sales of narcotics, and/or were laundered through U.S. bank accounts; on at least 64 occasions undercover operatives of Drug Enforcement Agency (DEA) operation were directed by criminal defendants to pick up large sums of drug proceeds, deposit them into U.S. bank accounts and wire the deposited money to U.S. or foreign bank accounts and each step in the receipt and laundering process was documented by the DEA operation and verified by Internal Revenue Service (IRS) special agent who worked with the DEA operation. U.S. v. Proceeds of Drug Trafficking Transferred To Certain Foreign Bank Accounts, D.D.C.2010, 757 F.Supp.2d 24. Controlled Substances ⊂= 184

Over $200,000 of currency found in automobile would be forfeited, as proceeds of drug transactions, despite claim of ownership made by passenger; sum was far in excess of what would normally be found in automobile, passenger had been found in Florida with substantial amount of currency in automobile and admitted to authori-

5. Black's Law Dictionary

Black's Law Dictionary is the most authoritative law dictionary ever published and the most widely cited legal reference in the world. Completely revised in 2014, the 10th Edition defines more than 50,000 terms and contains law-related abbreviations and acronyms, pronunciation guidance, and Latin maxims to guide anyone doing legal research.

Problem

What is the doctrine of "res ipsa loquitur"?

Black's Law Dictionary®

Tenth Edition

Bryan A. Garner
Editor in Chief

THOMSON REUTERS™

residue. (14c) **1.** Something that is left over after a part is removed or disposed of; a remainder. **2.** See *residuary estate* under ESTATE (3).

residuum (ri-**zij**-oo-əm). (17c) **1.** That which remains; a residue. **2.** See *residuary estate* under ESTATE (3). Pl. **residua** (ri-**zij**-oo-ə).

residuum rule. (1926) **1.** *Criminal procedure.* The doctrine that although hearsay is admissible at a probation or parole-violation hearing, some legal evidence (a "residuum") must be introduced to support a finding adverse to the defendant. **2.** *Administrative law.* The principle that an agency decision based partly on hearsay evidence will be upheld on judicial review only if the decision is founded on at least some competent evidence. • The residuum rule has generally been rejected by federal and state courts.

resign, *vb.* (14c) **1.** To formally announce one's decision to leave a job or an organization <to resign from the army>. **2.** To give up or give back (an office, trust, appointment, etc.) to those by whom it was given; to surrender <the officer resigned his commission>. **3.** To abandon the use or enjoyment of; to give up any claim <the monk resigned his inheritance>.

resignation, *n.* (14c) **1.** The act or an instance of surrendering or relinquishing an office, right, or claim. **2.** A formal notification of relinquishing an office or position; an official announcement that one has decided to leave one's job or organization, often in the form of a written statement. **3.** *Hist.* The surrender to the lord of the vassal's interest in land. — **resign,** *vb.*

resile (ri-**zIl**), *vb.* (16c) **1.** To retract (a statement, allegation, etc.). **2.** To draw back (from an agreement, contract, etc.). **3.** To return to one's original position.

res immobiles (rays i-**moh**-bə-leez), *n. pl.* [Latin] (18c) *Civil law.* Immovable things; chattels real. See IMMOBILIA.

res incorporales (rays in-kor-pə-**ray**-leez), *n. pl.* [Latin] (18c) *Civil law.* Incorporeal things; intangible things that are not perceptible to the senses. See *incorporeal thing* under THING.

res in privatorum patrimonio. See RES PRIVATAE.

res integra (rays **in**-tə-grə *also* in-**teg**-rə). [Latin "an entire thing"] See RES NOVA.

res inter alios. See RES INTER ALIOS ACTA.

res inter alios acta (rays **in**-tər **ay**-lee-ohs **ak**-tə). [Latin "a thing done between others"] (17c) **1.** *Contracts.* The common-law doctrine holding that a contract cannot unfavorably affect the rights of someone who is not a party to the contract. **2.** *Evidence.* The rule prohibiting the admission of collateral facts into evidence. — Often shortened to *res inter alios.*

"Res inter Alios; *facts not directly in issues, nor relevant thereto as above stated, are inadmissible.* — All facts not in issue themselves, and not connected with some fact in issue, or relevant thereto in some one of the above four ways, namely, either as forming part of the same transaction or subject matter; or as constituting a probable cause for it; or as the natural effect of it; or as necessary to explain or introduce it, are inadmissible in evidence for the purpose of forming the ground of an inference that such fact in issue or relevant fact probably did or did not exist, and are frequently designated, somewhat loosely, by the term, *res inter alios*, a phrase originally derived from the maxim *res inter alios, acta alteri nocere non debet,* but which is often used by the bench and bar in the sense of

irrelevant. This principle, that courts are not at liberty to infer from one fact the probable existence or nonexistence of another fact merely because the two are similar, unless they can be first shown to be part of the same transaction, or to be connected together in some way by the chain of cause and effect, is one of the most distinguishing characteristics of the English law of evidence." William Reynolds, *The Theory of the Law of Evidence* § 12, at 14–15 (2d ed. 1890).

res in transitu (**rays** in **tran**-si-t[y]oo). [Latin] *Hist.* Thing in transit.

res ipsa loquitur (rays **ip**-sə **loh**-kwə-tər). [Latin "the thing speaks for itself"] (17c) *Torts.* The doctrine providing that, in some circumstances, the mere fact of an accident's occurrence raises an inference of negligence that establishes a prima facie case; specif., the doctrine whereby when something that has caused injury or damage is shown to be under the management of the party charged with negligence, and the accident is such that in the ordinary course of things it would not happen if those who have the management use proper care, the very occurrence of the accident affords reasonable evidence, in the absence of the explanation by the parties charged, that it arose from the want of proper care. • The principle does not normally apply unless (1) the occurrence resulting in injury was such as does not ordinarily happen if those in charge use due care; (2) the instrumentalities were under the management and control of the defendant; and (3) the defendant possessed superior knowledge or means of information about the cause of the occurrence. — Often shortened to *res ipsa.*

"The phrase 'res ipsa loquitur' is a symbol for the rule that the fact of the occurrence of an injury, taken with the surrounding circumstances, may permit an inference or raise a presumption of negligence, or make out a plaintiff's prima facie case, and present a question of fact for defendant to meet with an explanation. It is merely a short way of saying that the circumstances attendant on the accident are of such a nature as to justify a jury, in light of common sense and past experience, in inferring that the accident was probably the result of the defendant's negligence, in the absence of explanation or other evidence which the jury believes." Stuart M. Speiser, *The Negligence Case: Res Ipsa Loquitur* § 1:2, at 5–6 (1972).

"It is said that *res ipsa loquitur* does not apply if the cause of the harm is known. This is a dark saying. The application of the principle nearly always presupposes that some part of the causal process is known, but what is lacking is evidence of its connection with the defendant's act or omission. When the fact of control is used to justify the inference that defendant's negligence was responsible it must of course be shown that the thing in his control in fact caused the harm. In a sense, therefore, the cause of the harm must be known before the maxim can apply." H.L.A. Hart & Tony Honoré, *Causation in the Law* 419–20 (2d ed. 1985).

"Res ipsa loquitur is an appropriate form of circumstantial evidence enabling the plaintiff in particular cases to establish the defendant's likely negligence. Hence the res ipsa loquitur doctrine, properly applied, does not entail any covert form of strict liability. . . . The doctrine implies that the court does not know, and cannot find out, what actually happened in the individual case. Instead, the finding of likely negligence is derived from knowledge of the causes of the type or category of accidents involved." Restatement (Third) of Torts § 15 cmt. a (Discussion Draft 1999).

res ipsa loquitur test (rays **ip**-sə **loh**-kwə-tər). (1962) A method for determining whether a defendant has gone beyond preparation and has actually committed an attempt, based on whether the defendant's act itself would have indicated to an observer what the defendant

Words and Phrases gives you definitions as construed by judges in case law. It is a good source to find how a word or phrase is defined in a specific factual context.

Problem

Find cases that involve the doctrine of "ejusdem generis" and compare how the term is defined in other contexts.

You can look either in the general Words and Phrases set (containing definitions from both federal and state cases) or in a Words and Phrases volume that accompanies a specific Digest set. An example from the general set is found at page 67. An example from the West's Federal Practice Digest is found at page 69.

The Words and Phrases set and digests will include "pocket parts" for recent material added since the time that the bound volume was last recompiled. A "pocket part" is a pamphlet tucked into the inside back cover of a bound volume. Always check the "pocket part" for the most recent cases. An example from a Words and Phrases pocket part containing definitions of "ejusdem generis" can be found at page 71.

WORDS AND PHRASES™

PERMANENT EDITION

Volume 14

E — EMERGENCY

Updated by cumulative annual pocket parts

THOMSON

™

WEST

Mat #40326704

R.I. 1943. "Ejectment" only lies where the ejector possesses the legal title.—Paliotta v. Celletti, 30 A.2d 108, 68 R.I. 500.—Eject 9(2).

Va. 1990. "Ejectment" is action to determine right and title of possession to real property. Code 1950, §§ 8.01–131 to 8.01–165.—Sheffield v. Department of Highways and Transp., 397 S.E.2d 802, 240 Va. 332.—Eject 1.

Wash. 1950. Where lessor was already in possession and did not seek to quiet title to land in his action against lessees to recover damages because of alleged improper methods of farming leased lands, action was not a suit for "ejectment" pursuant to statute. Rem.Rev.Stat. § 785.—Woodward v. Blanchett, 216 P.2d 228, 36 Wash.2d 27.—Land & Ten 280.

EJECTMENT BY FORCE

La.App.Orleans 1940. Where a lessor padlocks premises and thus prevents their use by the lessee, there results, in effect, an "ejectment by force."—Reed v. Walthers, 193 So. 253.

EJECTMENT SUITS

Tenn. 1925. Suits held properly appealed to Supreme Court as "ejectment suits" within meaning of statute.—Bouldin v. Taylor, 275 S.W. 340, 152 Tenn. 97.—Courts 246.

EJIDOS

Cal. 1860. "Suertes" is a term used in the Spanish law, to designate lots within the limits of cities, pueblos, or towns used for the purpose of cultivation or planting as gardens, vine-yards, orchards, etc. It is distinguished from "solares," which are smaller lots on which houses, etc., are built, and from "ejidos," which are in the nature of commons.—Hart v. Burnett, 15 Cal. 530.

EJUSDEM GENERIS

U.S. 2001. Under rule of "ejusdem generis," where general words follow specific words in statutory enumeration, general words are construed to embrace only objects similar in nature to those objects enumerated by preceding specific words.— Circuit City Stores, Inc. v. Adams, 121 S.Ct. 1302, 532 U.S. 105, 149 L.Ed.2d 234, on remand 279 F.3d 889, certiorari denied 122 S.Ct. 2329, 535 U.S. 1112, 153 L.Ed.2d 160.—Statut 194.

U.S.Cal. 1950. Ordinarily, rule of "ejusdem generis" limits general terms which follow specific ones to matters similar to those specified.—U.S. v. Alpers, 70 S.Ct. 352, 338 U.S. 680, 94 L.Ed. 457.— Statut 194.

U.S.Mo. 1934. Rule of "ejusdem generis" is applied as aid in ascertaining intention of Legislature, not to subvert it when ascertained.—State of Texas v. U.S., 54 S.Ct. 819, 292 U.S. 522, 78 L.Ed. 1402.—Statut 194.

U.S.Tex. 1941. The rule of "ejusdem generis" is applied as an aid in ascertaining the intention of the Legislature and not to subvert it when ascertained, and the rule gives no warrant for narrowing alternative provisions which the Legislature has adopted with the purpose of affording added safeguards.—U.S. v. Gilliland, 61 S.Ct. 518, 312 U.S. 86, 85 L.Ed. 598.—Statut 194.

U.S.Wash. 1975. Ordinarily rule of "ejusdem generis" limits general terms which follow specific matters similar to those specified but it may not be used to defeat obvious purpose of legislation.—U. S. v. Powell, 96 S.Ct. 316, 423 U.S. 87, 46 L.Ed.2d 228, on remand 537 F.2d 371.—Statut 194.

C.A.D.C. 1998. When a general term follows a list of specific terms, the rule of "ejusdem generis" limits the general term as referring only to items of the same category.—U.S. v. Espy, 145 F.3d 1369, 330 U.S.App.D.C. 299, on remand 23 F.Supp.2d 1.—Statut 194.

C.A.2 1991. Under the rule of "ejusdem generis," when general word follow the enumeration of particular classes in a statute, the general words should be construed as applying only to things of the same general class as those enumerated.—Samuels, Kramer & Co. v. C.I.R., 930 F.2d 975, certiorari denied 112 S.Ct. 416, 502 U.S. 957, 116 L.Ed.2d 436.—Statut 194.

C.A.9 2005. According to the canon of "ejusdem generis," a general term in a statute should be defined in light of the specific examples provided.— California State Legislative Bd., United Transp. Union v. Department of Transp., 400 F.3d 760.— Statut 194.

C.A.11 1984. Rule of "ejusdem generis" states that when there is, in same statute, a particular enactment, and also a general one which, in its most comprehensive sense, would include what is embraced in the former, particular enactment must be operative, and general enactment must be taken to effect only such cases within its general language as are not within provisions of particular enactment.—Estate of Flanigan v. Commissioner, Internal Revenue, 743 F.2d 1526.—Statut 194.

C.A.Fed. 1999. The rule of "ejusdem generis" calls for the tariff classification of imported articles with exemplars with which they share the same essential characteristics or purposes that unite the listed exemplars, but a classification is inappropriate when an imported article has a specific and primary purpose that is inconsistent with that of the listed exemplars in a particular heading.—Avenues in Leather, Inc. v. U.S., 178 F.3d 1241.—Cust Dut 17.

C.A.Fed. 1995. Under rule of "ejusdem generis," which means "of the same kind," where enumeration of specific things is followed by general word or phrase, general word or phrase is held to refer to things of same kind as those specified; as applicable to classification cases, ejusdem generis requires that imported merchandise possess essential characteristics or purposes that unite articles enumerated eo nomine, or by name, in order to be classified under general terms.—Totes, Inc. v. U.S., 69 F.3d 495.—Cust Dut 17.

C.A.Fed. 1994. Under rule "ejusdem generis," which means of the same kind, where enumeration

WEST'S
FEDERAL PRACTICE
DIGEST 4th

Volume 107

WORDS AND PHRASES
Cs — Ew

ST. PAUL, MN

WEST GROUP

or petition and insurance policy in determining whether insurer has duty to defend its insured in underlying suit; factual basis of determination should be established solely by allegations of pleadings filed in underlying suit, and facts outside pleadings are not considered.—Thomas J. Sibley, P.C. v. National Union Fire Ins. Co. of Pittsburgh, Pa., 921 F.Supp. 1526.—Insurance 2915.

N.D.Tex. 1995. "Eight corners rule" or "complaint allegation rule" requires court to examine only allegations in third party's pleading and insurance policy to determine whether duty to defend exists under Texas law.—Maryland Cas. Co. v. Texas Commerce Bancshares, Inc., 878 F.Supp. 939.—Insurance 2914.

S.D.Tex. 1996. Under "eight corners rule" or "complaint allegation rule" for determining insurer's duty to defend under Texas law, court takes allegations in underlying complaint as true, and duty arises if complaint asserts claim that is facially within terms of policy's coverage.—Aetna Cas. and Sur. Co. v. Metropolitan Baptist Church, 967 F.Supp. 217.—Insurance 2914.

S.D.Tex. 1995. Under "eight corners rule" for determining duty to defend under Texas law, courts look to allegations in pleadings in light of policy provision without reference to truth or falsity of such allegations and without reference to what parties know or believed facts to be or without reference to legal determination thereof; under the rule, duty to defend only arises if allegations in pleadings are potentially covered by the policy.—Potomac Ins. Co. of Illinois v. Peppers, 890 F.Supp. 634.—Insurance 2914, 2915.

S.D.Tex. 1995. Under Texas law, court determining insurer's duty to defend its insured follows "eight corners rule," under which court looks only to pleadings and insurance policy at issue to determine whether duty to defend exists.—Acceptance Ins. Co. v. Walkingstick, 887 F.Supp. 958.—Insurance 2914.

S.D.Tex. 1995. Under Texas law, court determining insurer's duty to defend its insured follows "eight corners rule" under which court looks only to pleadings and insurance policy at issue to determine whether duty to defend exists.—American States Ins. Co. v. Hanson Industries, 873 F.Supp. 17.—Insurance 2914.

S.D.Tex. 1993. "Eight corners rule" under Texas law refers to court's focus on factual allegations in complaint and on policy terms at issue, not merely on legal theories asserted.—American Guarantee and Liability Ins. Co. v. Shel-Ray Underwriters, Inc., 844 F.Supp. 325.—Insurance 2914; Plead 34(1).

W.D.Tex. 1996. Under "eight corners rule" or "complaint allegation rule" for determining whether insurer has duty to defend under Texas law, allegations of complaint are taken as true, and duty to defend arises if complaint thus construed asserts claim facially within coverage of policy as reflected by its terms; insurer may look solely at pleadings without reference to facts outside pleadings to

make determination of whether there is duty to defend.—Bituminous Cas. Corp. v. Kenworthy Oil Co., 912 F.Supp. 238, affirmed 105 F.3d 656.—Insurance 2915.

85/15 RULE

C.A.10 (Kan.) 1998. Compliance by nonprofit educational organization operating postsecondary vocational institution with minimum eligibility requirements for certification as propriety institution of higher education eligible for federally-funded student financial aid under Title IV did not mandate certification by Secretary of Education, and Secretary could impose compliance with "85/15 rule," requiring proprietary institution of higher education to derive 15% of tuition revenues from nonfederal sources to be eligible for federally guaranteed financial aid programs, under Higher Education Act (HEA). Higher Education Act of 1965, §§ 481(b)(3), (c), 1201(a)(4), as amended, 20 U.S.C.A. §§ 1088(b)(3), (c), 1141(a)(4); 34 C.F.R. § 668.13(c)(4)(ii).—Mission Group Kansas, Inc. v. Riley, 146 F.3d 775.—Colleges 9.25(2).

EJUSDEM GENERIS

C.A.D.C. 1998. When a general term follows a list of specific terms, the rule of "ejusdem generis" limits the general term as referring only to items of the same category.—U.S. v. Espy, 145 F.3d 1369, 330 U.S.App.D.C. 299, on remand 23 F.Supp.2d 1.—Statut 194.

C.A.2 1991. Under the rule of "ejusdem generis," when general word follow the enumeration of particular classes in a statute, the general words should be construed as applying only to things of the same general class as those enumerated.—Samuels, Kramer & Co. v. C.I.R., 930 F.2d 975, certiorari denied 112 S.Ct. 416, 502 U.S. 957, 116 L.Ed.2d 436.—Statut 194.

C.A.Fed. 1999. The rule of "ejusdem generis" calls for the tariff classification of imported articles with exemplars with which they share the same essential characteristics or purposes that unite the listed exemplars, but a classification is inappropriate when an imported article has a specific and primary purpose that is inconsistent with that of the listed exemplars in a particular heading.—Avenues in Leather, Inc. v. U.S., 178 F.3d 1241.—Cust Dut 17.

C.A.Fed. 1995. Under rule of "ejusdem generis," which means "of the same kind," where enumeration of specific things is followed by general word or phrase, general word or phrase is held to refer to things of same kind as those specified; as applicable to classification cases, ejusdem generis requires that imported merchandise possess essential characteristics or purposes that unite articles enumerated eo nomine, or by name, in order to be classified under general terms.—Totes, Inc. v. U.S., 69 F.3d 495.—Cust Dut 17.

C.A.Fed. 1994. Under rule "ejusdem generis," which means of the same kind, where enumeration of specific thing is followed by general word or phrase, general word or phrase is held to refer to

WORDS AND PHRASES™

PERMANENT EDITION

Volume 14

E — Emergency

2013
Cumulative
Annual Pocket Part
Covering opinions 2005 to date

THE WEST DIGEST TOPIC NUMBERS WHICH CAN BE
USED FOR WESTLAW® SEARCHES ARE LISTED ON
PAGE III OF THIS POCKET PART.

Mat # 41501047

38

EIGHTH AMENDMENT PROPORTIONALITY PRINCIPLE

C.D.Cal. 2008. "Eighth Amendment proportionality principle," does not require strict proportionality between crime and sentence, but rather, forbids only extreme sentences that are grossly disproportionate to the crime. U.S.C.A. Const. Amend. 8.—Fonseca v. Hall, 568 F.Supp.2d 1110. —Sent & Pun 1482.

EITHER VIEWPOINT

M.D.N.C. 2006. Even if the "either viewpoint" rule applies in class action lawsuits based on diversity jurisdiction, claim for declaratory judgment relief must be evaluated on single plaintiff basis; i.e., as with each plaintiff's claim for monetary damages, each plaintiff's claim for declaratory relief must be held separate from each other plaintiff's claim from both plaintiff's and the defendant's standpoint. 28 U.S.C.A. § 1332.— Chandler v. Cheesecake Factory Restaurants, Inc., 239 F.R.D. 432.—Fed Cts 346.

EITHER VIEWPOINT RULE

M.D.N.C. 2006. Under the "either viewpoint rule," the amount-in-controversy requirement for diversity jurisdiction in cases involving equitable relief is satisfied if either the gain to the plaintiff or the cost to the defendant is greater than $75,000. 28 U.S.C.A. § 1332.—Chandler v. Cheesecake Factory Restaurants, Inc., 239 F.R.D. 432.—Fed Cts 360.

EJECTMENT

Fla.App. 4 Dist. 2012. "Ejectment" is an action at law for a person to recover possession of property from a second person possessing it in hostility to the first person's right.—Royal Palm Corporate Center Ass'n, Ltd. v. PNC Bank, NA, 89 So.3d 923, rehearing denied.—Eject 1.

Pa.Cmwlth. 2009. "Ejectment" is an action filed by a plaintiff who does not possess the land but has the right to possess it, against a defendant who has actual possession.—Borough of Ulysses v. Mesler, 986 A.2d 224.—Eject 1.

EJUSDEM GENERIS

C.A.2 2008. "Ejusdem generis" is an aid to statutory construction problems suggesting that where general words follow a specific enumeration of persons or things, the general words should be limited to persons or things similar to those specifically enumerated.—Rajah v. Mukasey, 544 F.3d 427, for additional opinion, see 544 F.3d 449, on remand Matter of Rajah, 2009 WL 4026418, petition for review dismissed 405 Fed. Appx. 547.—Statut 1160.

C.A.Fed. 2010. Under the rule of "ejusdem generis," which means "of the same kind," where an enumeration of specific things is followed by a general word or phrase, the general word or phrase is held to refer to things of the same kind as those specified.—Nielson v. Shinseki, 607 F.3d 802.—Statut 1160.

C.A.Fed. 2008. The principle of "ejusdem generis" requires anything falling under the general term "or the like" to possess the same essential characteristic of the specific enumerated articles; the phrase "or the like" means "the same, or very similar to."—Deckers Corp. v. U.S., 532 F.3d 1312, rehearing denied.—Statut 1160.

C.A.Fed. 2008. Principle of "ejusdem generis," requiring anything falling under the general term to possess the same essential characteristic of the specific enumerated term, is useful in interpreting provisions of Harmonized Tariff Schedule of the United States (HTSUS). Harmonized Tariff Schedule, HTSUS 0101.10.00 et seq.—Airflow Technology, Inc. v. U.S., 524 F.3d 1287, on remand 804 F.Supp.2d 1292.—Cust Dut 17.

C.A.7 (Ill.) 2011. Under the "ejusdem generis" principle of statutory construction, where general words follow specific words in a statutory enumeration, the general words are construed to embrace only objects similar in nature to those objects enumerated by the preceding specific words.—U.S. v. Johnson, 655 F.3d 594, rehearing and rehearing denied.—Statut 1160.

C.A.2 (N.Y.) 2007. "Ejusdem generis" is the statutory canon that where general words follow specific words in a statutory enumeration, the general words are construed to embrace only objects similar in nature to those objects enumerated by the preceding specific words.—Wojchowski v. Daines, 498 F.3d 99.—Statut 1160.

C.A.4 (N.C.) 2009. Under North Carolina's "ejusdem generis" canon of statutory construction, where general words follow a designation of particular subjects or things, the meaning of the general words will ordinarily be presumed to be, and construed as, restricted by the particular designations and as including only things of the same kind, character and nature as those specifically enumerated.—Pitt County v. Hotels.com, L.P., 553 F.3d 308.—Statut 1160.

C.A.3 (Pa.) 2012. Under Pennsylvania law, under the principle of "ejusdem generis," general expressions such as "including, but not limited to" that precede a specific list of included items should not be construed in their widest context, but apply only to persons or things of the same general kind or class as those specifically mentioned in the list of examples.—Post v. St. Paul Travelers Ins. Co., 691 F.3d 500.—Contracts 156.

C.A.5 (Tex.) 2009. Doctrine of "ejusdem generis" counsels that general words following an enumeration of particular or specific items should be construed to fall into the same class as those items specifically named.—In re Dale, 582 F.3d 568.—Statut 1160.

7.   West Reporter

West Reporter

The following pages are included to illustrate added features in many West case law reporters. They include in order:

1. Map of Federal Judicial Circuits
2. Judges of the United States District Courts
3. Table of Cases reported in this volume
4. Table of Cases arranged by regional circuit
5. Words and Phrases section for cases in this volume
6. Opinion with Synopsis and Headnotes
7. Key Number Digest for cases in this volume

West's
FEDERAL
SUPPLEMENT

Second Series
A Unit of the National Reporter System

Volume 942 F.Supp.2d

Cases Argued and Determined
in the

UNITED STATES DISTRICT COURTS

UNITED STATES COURT OF
INTERNATIONAL TRADE

and Rulings of the

JUDICIAL PANEL ON MULTIDISTRICT
LITIGATION

THOMSON REUTERS™

Mat # 41445255

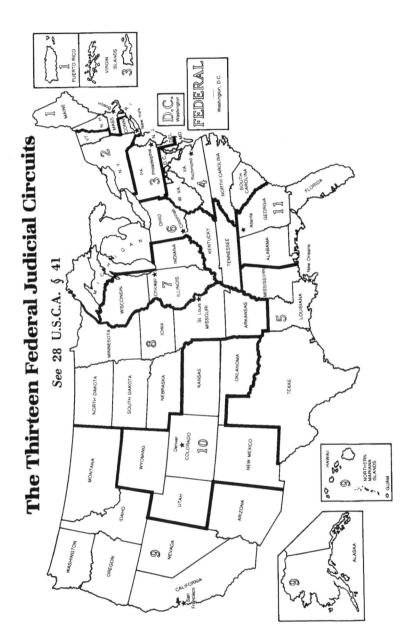

The Thirteen Federal Judicial Circuits

See 28 U.S.C.A. § 41

JUDGES
OF THE
UNITED STATES
DISTRICT COURTS

With Date of Appointment

DISTRICT OF COLUMBIA CIRCUIT
DISTRICT JUDGES

Royce C. Lamberth, C.J.	11-16-87	Washington
Emmet G. Sullivan	6-16-94	Washington
Colleen Kollar–Kotelly	5-12-97	Washington
Richard W. Roberts	7-31-98	Washington
Ellen Segal Huvelle	1-12-00	Washington
Reggie B. Walton	10-29-01	Washington
John D. Bates	12-20-01	Washington
Richard J. Leon	3-20-02	Washington
Rosemary M. Collyer	1-2-03	Washington
Beryl A. Howell	1-21-11	Washington
Robert L. Wilkins	3-1-11	Washington
James Emanuel Boasberg	4-1-11	Washington
Amy Berman Jackson	4-21-11	Washington
Rudolph Contreras	4-1-12	Washington
Ketanji Brown Jackson	4-18-13	Washington

SENIOR DISTRICT JUDGES

Louis F. Oberdorfer	11-1-77	Washington
Thomas F. Hogan	10-4-82	Washington
Gladys Kessler	6-16-94	Washington
Paul L. Friedman	6-16-94	Washington
Ricardo M. Urbina	6-16-94	Washington
Henry H. Kennedy, Jr.	10-20-97	Washington

FIRST CIRCUIT
DISTRICT JUDGES

John A. Woodcock, Jr., C.J.	6-27-03	Me.	Bangor
George Z. Singal	7-17-00	Me.	Portland
Nancy Torresen	10-11-11	Me.	Portland
Patti B. Saris, C.J.	11-24-93	Mass.	Boston
Rya W. Zobel	3-23-79	Mass.	Boston
William G. Young	4-4-85	Mass.	Boston
Douglas P. Woodlock	6-16-86	Mass.	Boston
Nathaniel M. Gorton	9-24-92	Mass.	Boston
Richard G. Stearns	11-24-93	Mass.	Boston
Nancy Gertner	2-14-94	Mass.	Boston

CASES REPORTED

CASES REPORTED

ARRANGED UNDER THEIR RESPECTIVE CIRCUITS

DISTRICT OF COLUMBIA CIRCUIT

FIRST CIRCUIT

SECOND CIRCUIT

XXXIII

WORDS AND PHRASES

For other judicial definitions,
see publication WORDS AND PHRASES.

ABUSE OF DISCRETION,
  Wilson v. Walgreen Income Protection Plan for Pharmacists and Registered Nurses, Walgreen Co., M.D.Fla., 942
    F.Supp.2d 1213.

ADVERSE,
  Flores v. Mamma Lombardis of Holbrook, Inc., E.D.N.Y., 942 F.Supp.2d 274.

ADVERSE EMPLOYMENT ACTION,
  McCullough v. Xerox Corp., W.D.N.Y., 942 F.Supp.2d 380.

AMBIGUOUS,
  Marzano v. Proficio Mortg. Ventures, LLC, N.D.Ill., 942 F.Supp.2d 781.

ARBITRARY AND CAPRICIOUS,
  Wilson v. Walgreen Income Protection Plan for Pharmacists and Registered Nurses, Walgreen Co., M.D.Fla., 942
    F.Supp.2d 1213.

ASSOCIATED-IN-FACT ENTERPRISE,
  Stitt v. Citibank, N.A., N.D.Cal., 942 F.Supp.2d 944.

AT THE WELL RULE,
  S Bar B Ranch v. Omimex Canada, Ltd., D.Mont., 942 F.Supp.2d 1058.

ATTORNEY,
  Davis v. Hollins Law, E.D.Cal., 942 F.Supp.2d 1004.

BY REASON OF,
  Gipson v. Popeye's Chicken & Biscuits, N.D.Ga., 942 F.Supp.2d 1303.

CLEARLY ESTABLISHED,
  Aranda v. City of McMinnville, D.Or., 942 F.Supp.2d 1096.
  Shearer v. Tacoma School Dist. No. 10, W.D.Wash., 942 F.Supp.2d 1120.

COMMERCIAL AVAILABILITY,
  Deacero S.A. de C.V. v. U.S., CIT, 942 F.Supp.2d 1321.

COMMISSION,
  Aranda v. City of McMinnville, D.Or., 942 F.Supp.2d 1096.

COMMUNITY CARETAKING DOCTRINE,
  Mateos-Sandoval v. County of Sonoma, N.D.Cal., 942 F.Supp.2d 890.

COMPELLED SELF-PUBLICATION,
  Byars v. School Dist. of Philadelphia, E.D.Pa., 942 F.Supp.2d 552.

CONCEPTION,
  Troy v. Samson Mfg. Corp., D.Mass., 942 F.Supp.2d 189.

CONCERTED ACTION,
  Byars v. School Dist. of Philadelphia, E.D.Pa., 942 F.Supp.2d 552.

CONFLICT OF INTEREST,
  Wilson v. Walgreen Income Protection Plan for Pharmacists and Registered Nurses, Walgreen Co., M.D.Fla., 942
    F.Supp.2d 1213.

CONTRARY TO,
  Ross v. Wolfe, D.Md., 942 F.Supp.2d 573.
  Melendez v. LaValley, S.D.N.Y., 942 F.Supp.2d 419.

DEFAMATORY,
  Byars v. School Dist. of Philadelphia, E.D.Pa., 942 F.Supp.2d 552.

ESSENTIAL FUNCTIONS,
  Anderson v. Georgia-Pacific Wood Products, LLC, M.D.Ala., 942 F.Supp.2d 1195.

Taylor GIPSON, Plaintiff,

v.

POPEYE'S CHICKEN & BISCUITS
et al., Defendants.

Civil Action No. 1:12–cv–03210–JOF.

United States District Court,
N.D. Georgia,
Atlanta Division.

April 22, 2013.

Background: Diabetic patron who used service dog to help him regulate his blood sugar level filed suit against Georgia restaurant, whose manager demanded that he leave restaurant because of his dog, and county, whose police officer asked him to comply with manager's demand, alleging they violated his rights under Americans with Disabilities Act (ADA) when he was asked to leave restaurant on account of presence of his service dog. County moved to dismiss.

Holding: The District Court, J. Owen Forrester, Senior District Judge, held that assuming that county police officer's response to scene, conversation with parties, and conveying to patron that restaurant was private property and that its manager could ask patron to leave, were "services, programs, or activities" under Title II of ADA, the exclusion, denial of benefit, or discrimination was not "by reason of" patron's disability.

Motion granted.

1. Civil Rights ⚷1053

In order to state claim under Title II of the ADA, plaintiff must show that (1) he is a "qualified individual with a disability," (2) he was either excluded from participation in or denied benefits of public entity's "services, programs, or activities," or was otherwise discriminated against by public entity, and (3) the exclusion, denial of benefit, or discrimination was by reason of his disability. Americans with Disabili-

ties Act of 1990, §§ 201(1), 202, 42 U.S.C.A. §§ 12131(1), 12132.

2. Civil Rights ⚷1053

Assuming, for purposes of motion to dismiss, that county police officer's response to scene, conversation with parties, and conveying to diabetic patron with service dog that restaurant was private property and manager could ask patron to leave, were "services, programs, or activities" within meaning of Title II of ADA, the exclusion, denial of benefit, or discrimination was not "by reason of" patron's disability. Americans with Disabilities Act of 1990, § 202, 42 U.S.C.A. § 12132.

> See publication Words and Phrases for other judicial constructions and definitions.

———

Allan Leroy Parks, Jr., Parks Chesin & Walbert, P.C., Parks Chesin & Walbert, Atlanta, GA, for Plaintiff.

Ogletree Deakins Nash Smoak & Stewart, Tampa, FL, Dara L. DeHaven, Lauren House Zeldin, Ogletree Deakins Nash Smoak & Stewart, P.C., Atlanta, GA, for Defendant, Popeye's Chicken & Biscuits, a/k/a Nashville Restaurant Management, LLC.

Deborah L. Dance, Mark Alan Adelman, Office of Cobb County Attorney, Law Department, Marietta, GA, for Defendant, Cobb County, Georgia.

ORDER

J. OWEN FORRESTER, Senior District Judge.

This matter is before the court on Defendant Cobb County's motion to dismiss [15].

KEY NUMBER DIGEST

ACTION

I. GROUNDS AND CONDITIONS PRECEDENT.

⊂⇒3. Statutory rights of action.

D.D.C. 2013. The Neutrality Act, providing for forfeiture to an informer of a share of vessels privately armed against friendly nations, but not expressly authorizing suits by an informer, did not create a private right of action that would allow a private citizen to bring an action against organizations that allegedly violated the act when they allegedly outfitted boats with supplies and arms in order to run an Israeli naval blockade with the alleged intent of supplying terrorist organizations; lack of an express cause of action within the statute indicated congressional intent not to provide one. 18 U.S.C.A. § 962.—Bauer v. Marmara, 942 F.Supp.2d 31.

When analyzing a statute to determine if it provides a private cause of action, the judicial task is to interpret the statute Congress has passed to determine whether it displays an intent to create not just a private right but also a private remedy.—Id.

The creation of private causes of action in the absence of an express legislative statement is disfavored.—Id.

Court would refrain from finding implied private right of action in Neutrality Act that provided for forfeiture to an informer of a share of vessels privately armed against friendly nations, but that did not expressly authorize suits by an informer, even though such a cause of action under the Act may have existed historically, where a lack of an express right of action indicated congressional intent not to create one, actions under the Neutrality Act implicated foreign policy which was the purview of the federal government, and forfeiture provided in the Act could only result from a criminal proceeding for which a private cause of action was extremely unlikely. 18 U.S.C.A. § 962.—Id.

Private rights of action are extremely unlikely to be found in statutory language customarily found in criminal statutes.—Id.

D.N.J. 2013. New Jersey Racing Commission's trainer-responsibility rule, which provided horse's trainer was "absolute insurer of and … responsible for [horse's] condition," did not create implied private right of action permitting racehorse owners to bring strict liability claims against trainer, or his employer under respondeat superior theory, to recover for quarantine imposed as result of outbreak of Equine Herpes Virus—Type 1 (EHV–1) that allegedly originated in employer's training facility; rule was promulgated to protect integrity of horse racing, not horse owners, and regulations specifically provided for rule's enforcement via administrative sanctions. N.J.A.C. 13:70–14A.6(a), 13:70–14A.7, 13:70–16.7.—New Jersey Thoroughbred Horsemen's Ass'n, Inc. v. Alpen House U.L.C., 942 F.Supp.2d 497, on reconsideration in part.

Under New Jersey law, in determining if an administrative regulation confers an implied private right of action, court considers whether: (1) plaintiff is a member of the class for whose special benefit the regulation was promulgated; (2) there is any evidence that the agency intended to create a private right of action under the regulation; and (3) it is consistent with the underlying purposes of the regulatory scheme to infer such a remedy.—Id.

II. NATURE AND FORM.

⊂⇒17. What law governs.

N.D.Cal. 2013. Under California's governmental interest choice of law test: (1) the court determines whether the relevant law of each potentially affected jurisdiction with regard to the particular issue in question is the same or different; (2) if different, the court examines each jurisdiction's interest in the application of its own law under the circumstances to determine whether a true conflict exists; and (3) if there is a true conflict, the court carefully evaluates and compares the nature and strength of each jurisdiction's interest in the application of its own law to determine which state's interest would be more impaired if its policy were subordinated to the policy of the other state.—Bias v. Wells Fargo & Co., 942 F.Supp.2d 915.

Ultimately, under California's governmental interest choice of law test, the court applies the law of the state whose interest would be more impaired if its law was not applied.—Id.

California's governmental interest choice of law test applies where there is no advance agreement on applicable law.—Id.

E.D.La. 2013. Under the Louisiana choice-of-law doctrine, the law of the state with a greater interest in the case will usually apply to substantive issues.—AGEM Management Services, LLC v. First Tennessee Bank Nat. Ass'n, 942 F.Supp.2d 611.

⊂⇒27(1). In general.

E.D.La. 2013. Under Louisiana law, the nature of the duty breached determines whether the action is in tort or contract.—AGEM Management Services, LLC v. First Tennessee Bank Nat. Ass'n, 942 F.Supp.2d 611.

For purposes of determining applicable prescriptive period, distinction between contractual and delictual damages under Louisiana law is that the former flow from an obligation contractually assumed by the obligor, whereas the latter flow from a violation of general duty owed by all persons.—Id.

III. JOINDER, SPLITTING, CONSOLIDATION, AND SEVERANCE.

⊂⇒43.1. —— In general.

E.D.Pa. 2013. Under Pennsylvania law, where evidence that would establish one complaint is distinct from evidence that would establish other complaint, complaints do not arise from same transaction or occurrence, as would warrant joinder. Fed.Rules Civ.Proc.Rule 18, 28 U.S.C.A.; Rules Civ.Proc., Rule 1020, 42 Pa.C.S.A.—Lehman Bros. Holdings Inc. v. Gateway Funding Diversified Mortg. Services, L.P., 942 F.Supp.2d 516.

(1)